"*B*eL *LR*in*gE*r"

A Lifetime in Athletics and Other Adventures

Jerry Pitts

Table of Contents

Dedication

My Lord and Savior, Jesus Christ

My parents, Leon and Willie Mae

Jim King, Head Coach, Livingston University

Dabbs Earnest, Coach, Sulligent High School

Leslie, My wife

Nathan, my son and Ashley, my daughter

About the Author

Born to Depression Era parents, Jerry Pitts spent over 50 years in athletics as a player, coach and administrator. Along with the experiences in athletics he also led a life filled with unusual, bizarre, and sometimes dangerous endeavors. He led a life that fulfilled most of his dreams as a boy which led to other outcomes that he could never foresee, of which, were the many strong relationships formed through the years and a personal relationship with Jesus.

Foreword

Bellringer!!

WOW!! What a great book that tells the story of my great friend, Jerry Pitts. This book follows Jerry's path as a young boy to high school sports star and on to an All-American football career at Livingston University.

Jerry and I were teammates at LU, coached high school football together and most importantly are lifelong friends.

Much of this book is devoted to the Livingston Tiger football team which rises from the depths to the very top of the small college football world, winning the 1971 National Championship and participating in the national playoffs 3 times from 1971-1975. This is the greatest era in the history of Tiger football.

This book tells the story of a football team that was an extension of a young and intense coaching staff. This staff knew the harder you worked the harder it was to give up. Not surprising, our coaches all went on to very illustrious careers.

Every player knew how hard every man had worked so believing in each other was not an issue. Coaches and players had worked too hard to let each other down.

Individual egos did not exist, laying it on the line for the sake of the team is what made our team unique.

The LU Tigers could abandon all doubt and trust absolutely without reservation that the player, beside, in front, and behind him would do exactly what it took to get the job done. Everyone had complete faith in each other and were in the same heartbeat, it is not unusual over 50 years later to hear teammates tell each other "Love you brother".

Jerry Pitts has done a wonderful job in capturing the identity of not only his team, but his family, his high school friends and teammates, and coaches, and putting his memories into words. Any sports fan would enjoy this book and traveling with Jerry as he travels from one stage of his life to another,

"Bellringer" – what a great description of Jerry Pitts. Coach Jim King knew exactly what he was doing when he gave Jerry this nickname. From experience I can tell you if you go against Jerry there is a good chance you were going to get your bell rung!!

"Bellringer" – brings back many great memories and follows the life of one of the very best!! An absolute must read.

Sam McCorkle

Sam McCorkle graduated from Meridian (MS) high school in 1968. He was a valuable member on two State football championships. He graduated from Livingston University in 1973 and was the starting center for the Tigers on their 1971 National Championship team and on the 1972 team that was defeated in the semifinals. Sam was the recipient of the "Phil Puccio Award" for leadership and dedication. He is the center on the Livingston University 1970's Team of the Decade.

Sam coached football for 47 years, 21 years as a head coach, 11 years as a college head coach in 6 different states and 4 SEC schools.

Introduction

My youngest memories are of those wanting to be a football player. Football was my idol at that time. This was at a very young age. The few games I was able to see on the black and white television, the occasional sports magazine, going to a few high school games, and having visions of games that had been played from stories told me from my dad, set the foundation for the love of football.

This is a sports book, but it is also a life book. It tells a unique journey that was molded, guided, effected, and honed by a lot of people. It tells of growing up without video games, without cell phones, with only 2 channels on the television. Growing up when I was 16 before we had air conditioning in the house and the first phone had five other families connected to the line and you had to take turns using it. There were not any fast-food establishments, but there were good home-grown vegetables accompanied by meat that we often raised ourselves.

It shows the importance of good role models in a youngster's life and great leaders later. It shows how I evolved from only wanting to play football to wanting to be the best in every sport I competed in. And I wanted to compete in any sport that involved a ball. I liked team sports better than individual ones, but I wanted to be the best individual on that team. Not for the glory, but my mindset was that if you are going to do something be the best. Of course, I was not the best in everything I tried, but that was ok too.

It tells of adventures that does not involve sports, but still had a great effect on my life. Sometimes being in the right place at the right time and sometimes the recipient of divine intervention. It solidifies my belief that leaders are made, not born and that actions can affect so many people and affect them in different ways. It also contains some very humorous events.

It contains love and faith, which are among the most important things in life.

Jerry Pitts

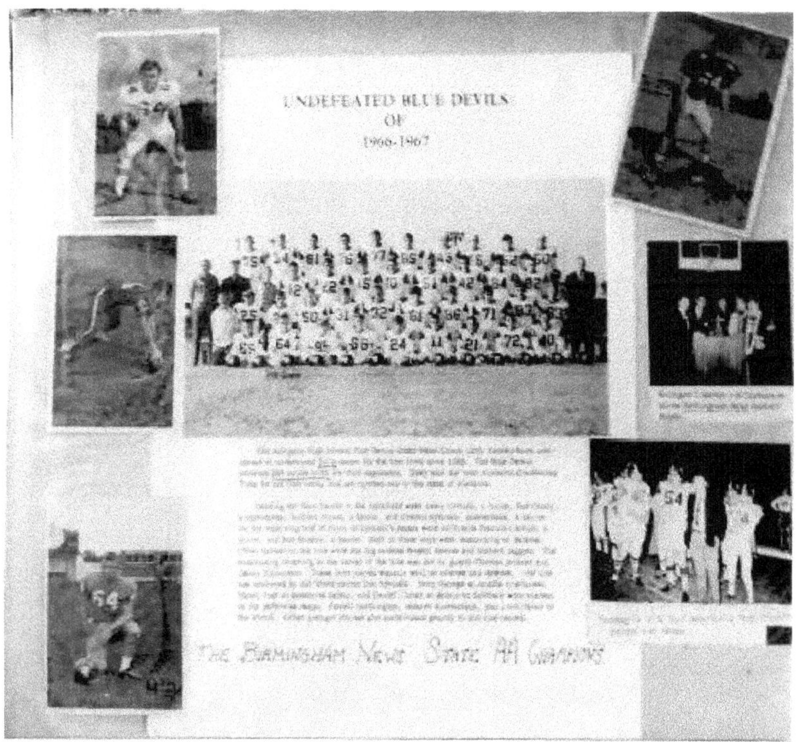

Winning championships is fun as a player……………

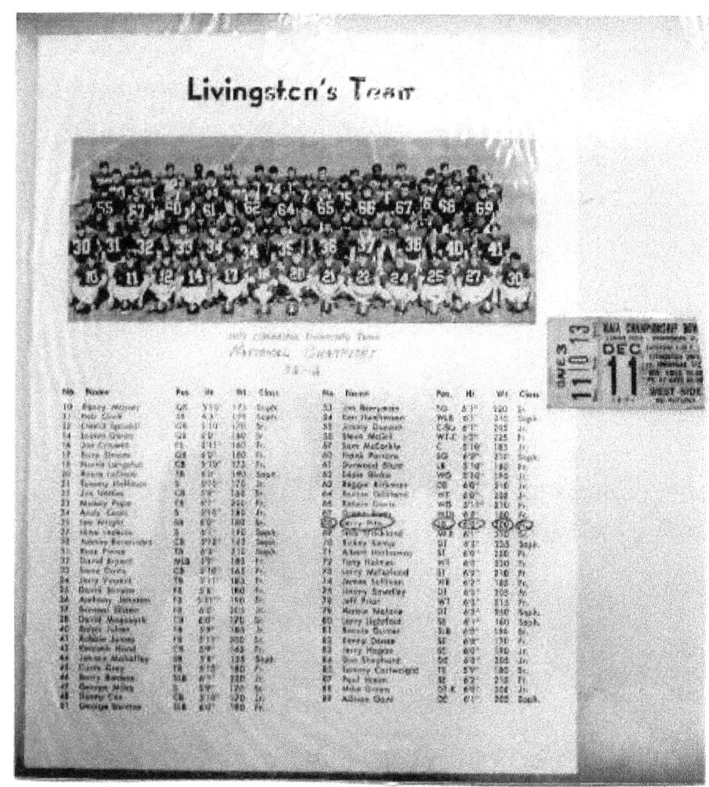

…….as a *Coach!!*

Chapter 1

Stranger Things

Home is where the heart is regardless of the name

Turd Bowl

As the end to the third week of fall practice in my first year at Livingston University approached its end, a strange question was being asked to the coaches by the upperclassmen. The question was "when is the first turd bowl going to be? What was a turd? Do not get me wrong, as a teenager I had used more than my share of profanity. However, not only had I never used that term, never had I heard it spoken. None of my high school coaches used profanity, but that changed 180 degrees at Livingston on the first day of practice. The other mysterious thing about the question was that when the upperclassmen asked the question they were smiling greatly and almost laughing. I had the feeling this turd bowl was not going to be a good thing for me. Finally, the head coach pronounced that the turd bowl would be the upcoming Saturday, which invoked much glee from the upperclassmen, especially the starters. I did not ask anyone what a turd bowl would be. I did not want to add to my list of anxieties.

Two days later at our team meeting before practice a somber group of coaches walked in and told the team that a beloved former player, Phil Puccio, had died in a car wreck. The players that knew him were devastated and I had a sad heart also because I could see how much he meant to them. A "Phil Puccio Award" would be established to designate what would be considered the Most Dedicated player on the team. I would later win that award after the 1974 season. The funeral was scheduled for Saturday so practice, and the turd bowl was cancelled.

The 1971 season was under way and we won the first two games. The defense was tremendous, and would be all season, but the offense was struggling. The opponent for the third week of the season would be Troy State University. A team Livingston rarely beat, and the one who would be our toughest remaining opponent that season. The game was played at Montgomery and was a brutal contest. Very physical. With about seven minutes to go in the game the Trojans had a 21-20 lead and we had just received the ball after a Troy punt inside of our ten-yard line. The offense began a methodical drive, converting several third down situations to keep the drive alive. With less than a minute remaining in the game the situation was fourth down and three yards to go. The offense had moved the ball to the Troy eight-yard line. A chip shot field goal wins the game. The kicker placed the tee down. In those days, an elevated block of plastic, about 2 inches high and four inches square would be used by the holder to put the ball on. Fans who have never played the game of football look upon this part of the game as something routine, when in fact it takes great skill to execute it. The center is snapping the ball knowing that he will be hit in the head, unprotected as soon as the ball moves. He has a small window of area to put the ball in. The holder must catch the spinning ball with one knee on the ground and the other leg bent at a 45-degree angle. If the snap is perfect it is usually an easy catch, but the holder must always be ready for a snap that could be left, right, high, or even bouncing to him. After the holder secures the ball, he must place it on the tee, lean it slightly backwards and spin the ball so that the laces of the football are on the opposite side of where the kickers foot will strike the ball. He must do this knowing that the kicker will be approaching the ball to kick it as soon as he sees the ball hit the holder's hands. Of course, the other eight players must block the opposing charging defensive players who are trying to block the kick. The Tigers are on the verge of a great victory. The snap, excellent, the catch and placement by the holder, excellent, the kick, BLOCKED!

Troy runs out the clock and we are devastated by the loss. It was impossible to tell what went wrong during the game, but after the coaches looked at the game film, they discovered that the kicker had placed the tee five yards behind the line of scrimmage instead of the required seven yards, this meant that when he kicked the football, he was so close to the defensive players that the ball did not elevate fast enough to get over the jumping defensive players.

The next week was an open week in which we did not have an opponent scheduled. The head coach and offensive assistant coaches knew that they needed to make a change on offense if we were going to have a successful season. The University of Alabama had made a change, secretly over the summer, from the I formation to the Wishbone offense. They had caught the University of Southern California completely off guard and had beat them 17-10 after losing to them by three touchdowns the previous season. Our head coach had played for Bear Bryant at Alabama and had called him to see if his assistant coaches and himself could drive to Tuscaloosa, only 60 miles from Livingston, learn as much as they could about the offense, and try to install it as the Tigers offense.

The previous seven weeks had been extremely demanding, both physically and mentally. Non-football students coming to campus and classes had only started a week earlier. Because of this the coaches decided to give the starters and others who had been playing a significant amount, both Monday and Tuesday off. These days were now reserved for Turd bowls. During the morning hours the offensive coaches would drive to Tuscaloosa to study the wishbone offense. Monday afternoon arrived and all freshmen, some sophomores and a few juniors assembled for practice. There were about 20 defensive players and 20 offensive players. Substitution and rest would be limited.

The offensive players had not been together as a group much. When they were together, they would be running the offense of the opposing team against our first team defense. This gave them a slight advantage as we, on defense, would be in the same defensive scheme that they were used to running against. However, offense takes a lot of timing with the different plays and blocking schemes. We ran a basic defense. Effective, but basic, which meant we could do less thinking and more full speed reacting.

We wasted little time in warming up before it was offense versus defense. All the coaches were still very pissed off at how the Troy Sate game went, especially at the end, and they were ready to vent some frustration. The offense ran three plays without getting a first down. They ran three more plays. No first down. This pattern continued for about an hour. The offensive coaches, especially the head coach, were furious. The defensive coaches acted like they wanted to be mad, but we were dominating the offense so much there was not much they could say. Secretly, I am sure they were enjoying what was happening. Finally, the head coach pronounces that if the offense did not get a first down on the next series that they would go to the end zone and run gasers. Now a "gaser" is when you line up in the end zone and run across the field sideways, completely to the other side, and back to your original spot. There was also a time limit involved in accomplishing this. The offense lined up. Three plays and no first down. True to his word, the head coach took the offensive players to the endzone and they ran five gasers. After a short break he pronounced that if they did not get a first down, they would be doing the same thing again. Three plays later, no first down, five more gasers. At this point there was not going to be any way the offense would get a first down, but the defensive coaches warned us that if they did, we would be doing gases. No one on defense was saying a word or mocking the offense.

The offense came to the line of scrimmage after their second round of gasers. The offense was running an "I" formation. In this formation there is a running back about three yards directly behind the quarterback and another running about two yards behind that running back. The running back that is closest to the quarterback is in a three-point stance while the other running back is standing up. When we looked into the eyes of the offensive players, we knew that they were close to total exhaustion. They got into formation and just before the snap of the ball, the running back in the down position jumped early which is a penalty. Without saying a word, the head coach runs to the player and uses a forearm on the back of the players helmet and knocks him to the ground. Almost instantly, the player grabs the coach by the collar and starts shaking him. The head coach now grabs the player by the front of his jersey, shaking him, and they make one roll with the head coach back on top saying, “someone had better get this SOB off me”. The player and coach are separated and in a turn of events that I, and probably almost everyone else did not expect, the coach says, “line up and run the play”! They again ran three plays, no first down. Practice ended shortly after.

The next day we had another turd bowl. The offense had a little success against us, but neither side had to run any gasers. These two practices helped me to get though the rest of the season because I knew if I could survive those practices, I could survive anything. Fortunately, those were the only two turd bowls we had that season.

Chasing Ken Stabler

Shortly after I was born in Montgomery, my parents moved to Birmingham for a period of time before permanently moving to Sulligent. My Daddy was raised in the Sulligent area. However, my Mother was on raised on the opposite end of the state. She was from a town smaller than Sulligent, She was from Repton located in Conecuh county, which bordered the Florida state line. IN the 50's and 60's there were not any interstates in Alabama and very few areas of 4 lane highways. It was a long trip between Sulligent and Repton. Not only did the distance make it long, but you had to travel through several towns, all with an abundance of traffic lights and stop signs. Cars were not air conditioned, did not get very good gas mileage, may or may not be able to pick up a radio station and could very easily break down or have a flat tire at any time. Because of these reasons we would only visit my grandparents in Repton 2.3. maybe 4 times a year.

So it was in the spring of 1967 that we headed toward Repton. In what was an unusual move, both of my parents had taken off from work on that particular Friday so that we would make the trip during the day and actually have a longer weekend. The trip was going like all the others, long and boring, especially for a 14-year-old. However, all of that was about to change.

A small town, Linden, was about halfway through our trip. This town had a lot of 4-way stops and a few traffic lights. They made for a slow journey through the town. The car in front of us didn't really catch anyone's attention in our family. However, it was a corvette, it was black, and it was a convertible. Enough of a nice car to take a second look, but not anything we had not seen before. The two passengers were young males. Obviously not high school students, but not much older than that. They were kind of cruising through the town, taking their time, and making our trip even slower. They seemed to be in a good mood as they were giving big waves to everyone they met, in cars or on the sidewalks. By the time had painstakingly made it through the last stop sign and traffic light and was outside the town limits my daddy was ready to get on down the road. He floored it.

Evidently, the passing of the corvette did one of two things for those guys in the corvette. It either made them mad that someone had passed them, or, and I believe this was the true reason, was that they were bored and were ready for some fun. To them that would be speed on the highway.

Most people know that Corvettes are built for speed. I need to explain the type of car my daddy was driving, It was a 1964 Ford Galaxie. It had a 427 cubic-inch engine under the hood. These cars had been designed for NASCAR and it was as powerful as any Corvette. My daddy had it ordered it special and in the specifications, he had 4-speed stick shift in the floorboard.

Now as my daddy was exceeding the speed limit, the corvette quickly caught up to us and was "riding our bumper", so to speak. When the first short open distance available for passing appeared the Corvette blew around us. I guess my daddy was also bored and quickly caught up with them. He soon returned the favor and passed them. This went back and forth with speeds reaching into the 90 mph and plus range at times, I want to emphasize that this race was taking place on a two lane highway with plenty of curves, curves sometimes used as passing lanes. My mother was very upset, as one of her biggest phobias in life was dying in a car wreck. My sister and I just watched the event unfold since we had confidence in whatever our daddy did.

30 miles later, and I don't remember the time late but I know it was less than 30 minutes later, was the town of Thomasville, At this particular junction of the race the Corvette was in the lead. They had slowed down to the posted speed limit inside the city limit and my daddy wasn't going to pass them there. The Corvette then pulled into a gas station and daddy followed them in. He said he was going to talk to them a bit, probably car stuff, as he was also a mechanic, among other things. I went to the restroom.

Just as I exited the restroom my daddy headed toward me with a glow on his face, a lively step, and excitement in what he was about to tell me. He told me to come with him to meet the guys we had been racing. As we went to the driver's side he said, "meet Ken Stabler"! I was in shock and in awe! Stabler was the best known player/celebrity that I had ever met in my young life. Yes, I had captured some autographs from professional athletes, but had not had the experience of a truly one-on-one conversation that I was now having with one of the true greats of college football. He was very nice. Very down to earth. And of course, I got his autograph.

Later it was revealed that Stabler was driving the Corvette although he was extremely poor. Surprised? Don't be. He had persuaded a car dealership to basically give him the car by promising the sales staff he would soon be a professional athlete and that it would be good publicity for them after his eligibility was completed.

And why was Stabler able to drive home during the spring when the rest of his teammates at Tuscaloosa were having spring football practice? Coach Bear Bryant had suspended Stabler for “non-conformity to team rules”. As I am sure you know if you are a football fan, whatever Stabler had to do to get back on the team he did it, as he led the Crimson Tide to an 8-2-1 season I n1967,

One of the best car races in history!

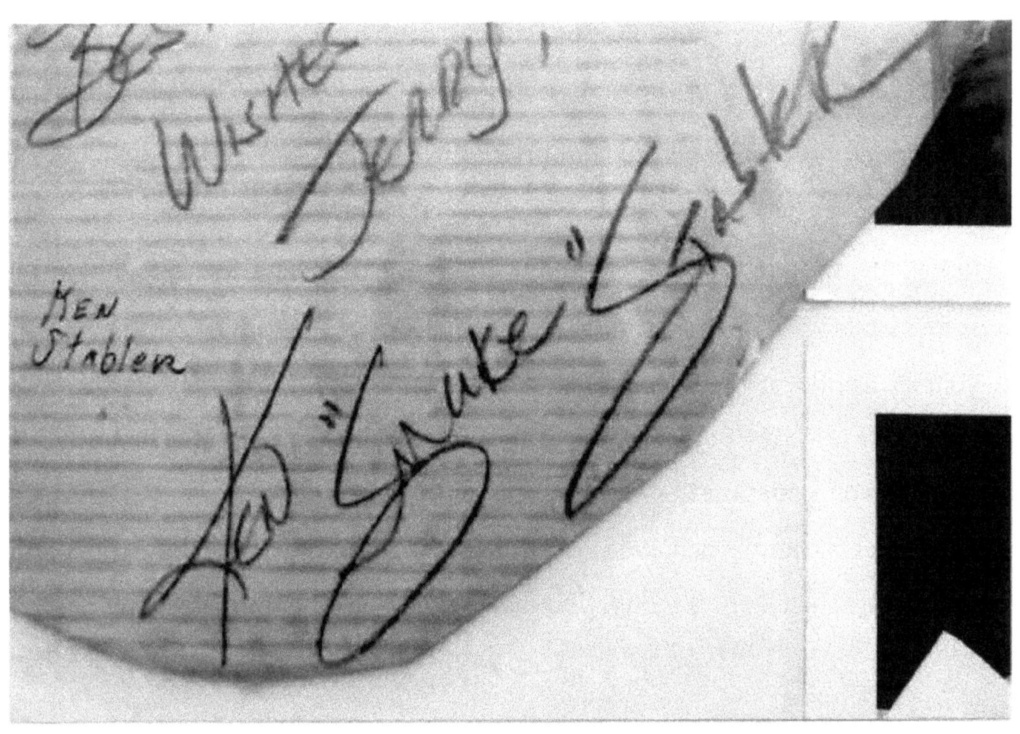

Ken Stabler's Autograph

On the sideline

Creative Motivation

One thing about coaches is that they are always looking for an edge. All good coaches know that it takes talented players, good preparation during practice, and a good plan and execution of that plan to win games. However, there are always intangibles that may make a difference in the outcome of a game, especially when the opponents are evenly matched.

One of those intangibles is motivation. You usually start with pride as a motivational factor. Pride in yourself, pride in the team, pride in the community. After that coaches can get very creative. One of those avenues of creativity is the area of making your players mad at the opponent. This can be achieved sometimes by the way the opponent has beaten you the previous time that you played them. This can be achieved sometimes just by the fact that the opponent has always been a natural rival. Then there is motivation that is used in the hopes of creating rage against your opponent.

Now I can't say exactly who was involved in these creative motivational techniques that took place but I'm pretty sure all of them came from "in-house". Now when one is in the 16-18 year old range, one is still gullible, You want to believe that what your coach tells you is the gospel. These creative motivational techniques usually take place very close to the time of the contest. In fact, all of the ones that involved me as a player took place the day of the contest and sometimes even right before kickoff. By using the word kickoff you probably surmise that all of those creative motivational techniques occurred before football games. You are right if you did.

The first occurred when I was a freshman. Sulligent was playing Guin in what was going to be a close game. Sulligent went undefeated the season before and was named 2A State Champions by the Birmingham News. We lost several good players, but had a good bit of talent returning. After warming up we returned to the dressing room. The game was at Guin. Players gathered around for the traditional last-minute pep talk by the head coach. All of the sudden he appeared holding a piece of poster paper and in a semi-rage. I don't remember the exact drawing on the poster board but I do remember it was a very disrespectful image of our mascot, Blue Devil, being pounded by a Red Raider Chief. Coach had "found it" somewhere in the locker room in between the time we had went out to warm up and the time we had returned. We had been disrespected in the most ultimate way. We should be very anger with the intent of inflicting great pain on our opponent. At least that is what the coach was saying and, as much, we bought into that.

We got beat. The game was close. They made a few more plays than we did.

Other creative motivational techniques over the years were the painting of disrespectful sayings on the side of our field house and gym and the sending of black roses to us by our opponent. Some of these games we won, some, we lost. After I started playing college football and as I got into my coaching career I found out that last minute motivational talks, or actions, especially the "creative" ones did very little to affect the outcome of a game. Motivation was best used when it was fed to the players a little at a time during each day of practice. Pep talks right before game time is better used to remind players of the roles and responsibilities instead of false emotion that will soon fade away. Emotion needs to be built during the week for it to last an entire game.

I will smile when I think of some of these creative motivational techniques I experienced. The main thing is that the coaches were working hard for a win and I still admire them for that extra effort.

Basketball Practice – Shorts Only

One thing is for sure. If anyone ever believed in basketball being a "team" game and that there was any room for individualism it was Coach Dabbs Earnest. I will talk about him in more detail in another chapter, but we all found out about this philosophy of his on the first day of basketball practice during his first year as coach at Sulligent.

Practice for the 1968-69 season started on a Monday following the last football game the previous Friday. All of the players were in a small meeting room in the gym waiting for Coach Earnest. When he enters the room all of us almost break out in laughter until we see the seriousness on his face. Since Coach Earnest moved to Sulligent about 6 months earlier, he had a head full of wavy hair. Not long but enough to be considered a normal length. However, at some point between the last football game on Friday and to this moment of entrance, he had visited a barber shop. He now sported a "flat-top" that was all but shaved on the sides with a little hair sticking up in front. No one commented on it.

That was our first indication of his seriousness toward the sport of basketball. There were some other details that would emphasize that point, but the main one would be our practice uniform. Our practice uniform consisted of a pair of white shorts. Tennis shoes and white socks of course, but other than that, white shorts. No Tops! We were all equal in that extent. It was a move no one expected, but in an attempt to build a "team", this was his first move. In my opinion it was a spectacular move. It was humbling, it built cohesiveness, and it separated the players from him, in that he was "in charge", and we were his building blocks for a successful program.

When we scrimmaged, the five on defense would wear a very thin mesh blue top so that there wouldn't be any confusing relate to offense and defense. We would have his attire as our practice uniform for the three yeas that I played for him.

6th Grader on the Junior High Team

For years I played backyard football. I played with classmates at school, and I played with ghosts at home. The imagination of a young boy who wanted to be great at football did not have any boundaries when I the yard on green grass with a brown football. Time was my enemy as I could only dream of putting on an official uniform and lining up between fans on my side and fans of the opposing team. I had watched a movie that was a football tale of boys my age and younger playing organized football. It wasn't fair. So far, the closest thing that I had gotten to any point of organized football was when the local Ford dealership sponsored the NFL Punt, Pass, and Kick contest. I didn't do very well, but I was able to keep a card that had the official NFL logo! Of course, it was pinned on my wall where it was the last thing I saw before I went to bed and the first thing I saw when I woke up.

In 1964, in Sulligent, there was not any such thing as Toy Bowl, Pee Wee, or any other name of organized youth football. There was only a rush to the field during recess at school to play and my "friends" waiting at home. I don't know how it happened. I don't even remember who I talked to. Of course, I had to have talked to my parents and the junior high coach. I know I just didn't show up one day, but I played on the junior high team as a 6th grader. To explain what Junior High team means is that it was made up of boys from the 7th, 8th, and 9th grades. Usually there were more 8th and 9th graders than 7th graders. There were 2 coaches, one that was part of the school system and a volunteer from the community. They would have their own dressing area. I stress "dressing area" because I don't want you to think of anything fancy like a field house. The equipment was hand-me downs that was once used, and almost used up, by the varsity. They usually played somewhere between 6-8 games.

There are only two things I remember about that season. One is that before the first practice I had a player who was in the 8th grade telling me that "those guys" were going to kill me. I don't know if he told me that because he really believed it or that at 110 pounds, I was already bigger than him.

The other thing was the "Moon Pie/RC Cola incident". Without a doubt the Vernon Bulldogs, 10 miles from us, were our biggest rivals in all sports, but it was even more vicious in football. Think Alabama/Auburn, Ohio State/Michigan, USC/Notre Dame, and you will understand the intensity of Sulligent/Vernon.

It was an afternoon contest in the middle of September. In front of the Vernon student body and a few adults who were not working or retired. This meant that we were greatly outnumbered, fan support wise. It was hot. It was 90 degrees plus hot. It was also a day after a big rain had come through the area. The field was sloppy and had a sour smell that comes from the mixture of mud and heat. I'm not sure what the score was but I know we were not winning. The scene is as real now as it was then. All the players were in a semicircle on one knee. A somewhat calm and subdued situation suddenly exploded. Whereas the junior high coaches were talking to a few players, the head coach, Coach Jenkins, was now front and center, and he was not happy. To be fair, happiness was not in his vocabulary, much less his personality during football season. However, what he had seen, or maybe it was what he hadn't seen, made him even less happy.

I'm not sure how long his rant lasted. To an eleven-year-old it seemed like an eternity, but it may have only been a few minutes. Regardless, he was getting his point across as stone-cold silence had engulfed everyone around him. I don't know if he talked about schemes, effort, concentration, intensity, or any other factor related to the game, but I do know he was issuing a warning about what would happen at practice the next day if he did not get what he wanted in the second half of the game.

To put a final emphasis on his tirade he issued an ultimatum. His exact words were, "If you don't like what I'm saying and if you don't want to do what I'm telling you, then you can go and join the RC Cola drinking and Moon Pie eating bunch and I don't care!" You see, in 1964 eating or drinking anything with sugar in it, other than your mom's home-made sweet tea was off limits. Evidently, RC Cola was the absolutely worst thing you could drink, and Moon Pies were absolutely the worst thing you could eat.

I do not remember anything about the second half of that football game. I don't know who won. I don't even know what happened the next day at practice. All I remember is that during that halftime, Zeus was raining down bolts of lightning on us and we barely made it out alive!

High School Travel for Basketball and Baseball Games

I guess, to the best of my knowledge, sometime during the 1970's the word "liability" creeped into the arena of high school sports. I think safety concerns for high school athletes, off the field, kind of evolved instead of one explosive moment.

Sulligent is in an area of high poverty. Not extreme poverty, but above the 50% level. It was about my sophomore season before a booster club was formed and there was not any such thing as fund raising activities. Today, there are fund raises going on constantly, and not just for athletics, but for FFA, Chorus, BETA, etc. SO in the past, athletics was funded almost strictly on money made from gate receipts. A big cost in the budget of each athletic team was travel. The football team was going to travel on a bus. That was a given. However, the varsity basketball and baseball teams had a different mode of travel – personal cars.

There would be the head coach driving his car. The assistant coach would be driving his car. They would each have somewhere between 4-5 players, depending on the size of the car, riding with them. After that, players, with a driving license, who had a car, and had parents that would let them drive, would be in the "train" going to and from games. Every school in our area traveled this way. No one ever thought anything about the dangers that were involved. Of course, the coaches would give us detailed instructions about how to drive, to stay in line, not passing each other, only passing other cars if the coach did first and then only when it was completely safe. Players even provided gas for their own cars and were not reimbursed.

Since the junior high teams obviously did not have anyone that could drive, they did ride in a small van that would seat around 10 people.

Times have changed and now all transportation of students for any event is by school bus with a driver that has a CDL and has been trained to drive a school bus. How lucky we were that no one ever had a wreck, ran out of gas, or even had a flat tire during all those trips.

It was not that all of these schools were too cheap to provide a bus, they just didn't have the money to do so back during that time.

Toilet Dunk

Was it harassment, hazing, class structure, hormones, learned behavior, or maybe it was becoming part of a team, a close-knit team? I guess it depends on who you ask and who was affected by it. It was upper classmen vs. freshmen. It was no contest. Most freshmen resisted with very little effort because resistance was futile. Even with this knowledge some "fought back". For the rest of us, their resistance was a good thing as they became a constant target.

Most of the hazing was usually in the form of minor physical pain. Belts were the most common instrument used when you failed to perform a task, usually a task that was not going to be to the satisfaction of those giving the command no matter how well it was performed. Most of the pain that was inflicted was so minor that it was gone within minutes. Most of those these are those that have been seen in movies or television shows over the years. Most were also not as severe as some that the entertainment industry has portrayed. However, one was carried out before practice one day that, to say the least, was not common.

It was boring in Livingston, before the school semester started, when you were not at practice, at a meeting, or in class. Football practice was not boring. I can say that I never witnessed or took part in a boring practice. The intensity level always begins to simmer in the locker room. Players knew that mental preparation was a must to survive. We all had the physical skills to survive, but it took more than that. At times, this "mental preparation" did more than simmer and morphed into a freshman getting some more orientation.

On one particular hot day, when a very physical practice awaited the team, two of the upper classmen who "enjoyed" helping the freshman become orientated, decided it would help team morale by directing the focus from the "practice schedule" that had been posted, to a locker room event. They recruited another upperclassman and headed toward the freshman who always offered the greatest resistance for them. Lost over the years is the memory of the exact conversation that took place, but the mental image is still very fresh. After some struggling, that continued unsuccessfully throughout the event, the event took place. The older guys had taken the freshman and turned him upside down. Yes, of the ground, head down, feet up in the air. The three were moving him from his locker toward a toilet. Well, as it turned out it was more than a "scare", it was a nightmare for the freshman. Being "considerate", one of the upperclassmen flushes the toilet.

When the water level rose back to normal the upperclassmen then put the head of the freshman into the water of the toilet and flushed again!

After standing the freshman up, while laughing, they were patting him on the back. Of course, the freshman was cursing them but that was his extent of any type of retribution. We all finished dressing, including the freshman, and headed toward the practice field. It took about ten minutes to walk to the practice field and by the time we got there no one was talking about what had happened because of what lay ahead.

I don't ever recall anyone talking about this event after that day. It just didn't seem tat important in the bigger scheme of things. The freshman that had just had his head dunked in a toilet, was always hanging around the ones that had dunked him. He never filed a complaint with the coaches, and Deans of the university, the Gulf South Conference, or the NCAA. He was part of something that was important to him and he was willing to pay a small price for that membership.

Leaving Equipment

High school football is a phenomenon that is rarely rivaled. It is like this bot in a positive and the negative. I the positive, when the local high school football team is doing well, the whole community is excited. People bring food for the players to eat, they come early for the games, and it is a "we" experience, If the season is going poorly the players eat on their own, the stadium may be half full, and it is a "they" thing.

The 1970 high school football season for Sulligent was majestic. Sulligent had won the 1966 State Class AA Championship named by the Birmingham News. It was a year before the Alabama High School Athletic Association implemented an on the field playoff system. The first three years involved only 4 teams from each of the 4 classes. However, in 1970, the AHSAA expanded the field to 8 teams.

Based on a point system it was determined that if we won our last game, we would finish at number 5 putting us in the playoffs, but if we lost, we would not be in the playoffs. Needless to say, a lot was riding on the final game. The final game was a road contest at Carbon Hill, some 45 miles away from Sulligent. We were favored but being a road game always presented possible problems.

As a team all the players wore ties to the game and dressed in their game equipment after arriving at the site. Each player packed his own equipment in a large cloth bag with a pull string. Everything that you would need to play a game was in that bag. During that era, coaches rarely brought extra equipment other than items that might need to be used to fix a face mask, some shoestrings, some tape, and a few medical items.

We ate our pregame meal. It was a perfect night for a football game. Cool enough for a light jacket, but without any wind or the threat of rain. The coaches planned for us to get to the opposing team's stadium an hour and half before the scheduled kickoff time. The bus ride would take close to an hour that would put us leaving around 4:30 that game. Everyone on the team was excited. We were ready to play. We had confidence and we knew that almost everyone who was a football fan in our small town would be there to watch us.

One of the most important rules that we had was that when traveling to a game there had to be absolute silence by the players on the bus. Most times this was not a problem for me because I knew focus was important for a football game. However, it was different tonight. I was focused but I was happy. We all were happy. We were feeding off each other's energy. It was hard to hold back smiles and not to look at other teammates. We knew we were going to win and go to the state playoffs.

What seemed like a two-hour ride was finally over. After stepping off the bus we knew we could have light conversations. The first thing we always did was to walk across the football field. This got the bus ride out of our system and gave you a feel for the turf you would be battling on. While we were walking the managers were putting the bags of equipment in the middle of the locker room floor. As we came into the locker room player after player would walk over to the pile, look through the bags until they identified their equipment and then pick out a place to get dressed.

I had come in about middle of the pack from the field and started looking for my bag. It was not a big deal that I could not find it immediately. However, after looking at 3 or 4 different bags, plus the fact that the pile was getting smaller. I had a slight bit of anxiety to come over me. That slight anxiety turned into full blown panic when I was left looking at a floor that did not have any more bags and I did not have mine in my hands. Total fear now gripped me as I looked around and saw all the other players getting dressed. That fear increased with the fact that none of them were pulling a prank on me and had hidden my bag. The ultimate fear had now frozen my body as I made eye contact with my coach and we both realized at the same time that I did not have my equipment bag.

As a senior in high school, you sometimes get filled with yourself and have to be brought back down to earth. This night was my night for that to happened. As a team we were having a great year and I was also individually. I packed my bag. I didn't leave anything out. I had told a manager to put it on the bus for me. Why did I tell him? Well, I went through a little entitlement period. I mean it was like 100 feet from where my bag was packed to the truck they were putting the equipment bags in. Other players were carrying their bags. Maybe a couple of other players had asked to get theirs, but mainly the players loaded their own bags. Managers had a lot of tasks to do.

I could barely audible the words needed to tell my coach what has happened. This was before cell phones. This was way before answering machines. By the time we had arrived almost everyone else that was coming to the game that had any connection to the school had left Sulligent. The first thing that happened was that my coach turned beet red with anger. Thankfully, he never used profanity, but what came out was almost as bad.

After enough time had elapsed for him to come back into reality he moved quickly. He located a phone from the opposing head coach and began calling people. No one was left. No one except one store merchant who had forgotten something and just happened to be at home when going back to retrieve it. My coach gave him some information about one of the doors on the gym that if you pulled it a certain way would come open. He told him where my equipment bag would be and asked him if he would get it and bring it. This man was a big fan of the school in general, not just the football team, and was more than glad to do it.

In the meantime, there was the pregame warmup. I was backed up, humble, like a wet dog. I was ashamed on several levels and was about to be more ashamed. Reluctantly our coach asked another player, slightly bigger than me, but one that did not start or play very often. To let me use his equipment to warm up. He did, with fussing, which embarrassed me even more. Going out to warm up everything shook just a bit. Nothing fit right and every step was a reminder of how foolish and selfish I had been. Warmups lasted about 45 minutes. I barely spoke and then just the necessary things that were required. I was not doing a lot of the normal yelling that usually went along with getting ready for a game. As we were returning to the locker room, I noticed the merchant that had been called was standing by the bus. My heart lifted. Inside was my bag of equipment. I quickly changed, gave my teammate his equipment, and sincerely thanked him.

We went onto easily win the game. By the time the fourth quarter came around my coach had somewhat put the issue behind and even let me play fullback for a few plays. It was a great feeling after the game. We all rode back together and as a surprise, team boosters had us a post-game meal waiting on us.

In hindsight, the coaches would have been justified not to have given me the other player's uniform. It wasn't his fault. They would have been justified not to start me. They would have been justified if they had not played me. I learned a valuable lesson that night. I learned it wasn't all about me.

High School Basketball Pre-game

Most athletes, and fans, know the term "pre-game". It is the period leading up to the actual contest and most people would consider that to be a 3-to-5-hour window of time. Lots of discussion has taken place on the issue because it is a fascinating aspect of athletics. What do you eat, how far in advance of the contest do you eat, do you nap, do you get by yourself or in a group, etc. It is interesting in that coaches, players, and fans are wondering what routine, if any, will give you an advantage over your opponent.

In high school our football pre-game was determined by the head coach. In basketball, because of finances, we, the players, determined our pre-game routine. The only thing we had to do, per instruction by the basketball coach, was to be at the gym by a predetermined time.

Of course, in high school, one of the driving forces for an athlete is food. Well, actually, when you are in high school, you do not have to be an athlete for one of your top priorities to be food. As soon as we were dismissed from school there were always four of us who went together to eat. Carlos, Mike, Jimmy, and myself. Sometimes another Mike would join us. We headed to "Leon's Grill" in Sulligent. A legendary place to eat. Leon Hollis was the owner and a man of many talents. Leon was a postal worker, barber, cook, mayor, and a person that had a very unique gift. Leon could "throw his voice", Now, you may or may not know what "throw your voice" means, but it is literally what it sounds like. Leon could be standing at one location and say something. However, you would not hear what he said if you were standing by him, but you would hear if you were further away. And when I mean away, I mean up to 100 feet away. He would not use this skill often, but to the "victim" it was truly frustrating.

We would never change our food orders. We didn't have the same exact orders, but we were consistent. Mine was two cheeseburgers, French fries, sweet tea, and for desert apple pie with vanilla ice cream on top. Yes, I was full when I finished. A bonus to this was I didn't even pay. My sweet, dear, mother, who toiled for many years in a garment factory would come by on Fridays to pay my tab. What a blessing to my life she was. Not because she paid for my food, but for the example she set in her hard, dedicated work life in which she sacrificed so much for her children.

After eating we all headed to Jimmy's house. It was the closest house to the school and would be empty for us. Now, you would think that after a big meal we would all be ready for a nap. No. We were too competitive to sleep. We were always finding ways to compete. Jimmy was more of a farmer/carpenter/ mechanical type person than the rest of us. He would take AG science every year and part of that involved welding. When welding, sometimes small, round pieces would form. These pieces would be about ¼ inch in diameter. He would bring some of those pieces with him and we would have a “hockey tournament”. WHAT?! We would use those pieces as pucks, butter knives as shafts, and plastic cups as goals. We would lie down on the floor and play hockey. And it was fierce, but fun. This would usually take up about an hour of our time after which we would take a short nap before heading to the gym.

Routine: Eat-Compete-Sleep-Be on time.

Shaved Heads

In 1971, bald heads, or should I say, shaved heads, were not I style, in fact, long hair was becoming the style. Long hair had yet to overtake the players on the Tiger football team, but all the players were proud of what they had. One of the reasons that they were proud of what they had was that at one point in the time since they had gotten to Livingston, they had all their heads shaved off. This ritual usually took place I August, during camp, before classes started. This usually gave those who had their heads shaved about 3 weeks of growing time before the arrival of other students.

As in most cases like this, it was upon the shoulders of the upper classmen to carry on this tradition. Since upperclassmen outnumbered freshmen 3 to1 there was not any doubt as to whether a freshman would get his head shaved. A lot of different situations had developed that had resulted in this event being pushed way into the season, late into the season, so late that cold weather had set in.

After a midweek practice, the upper classmen had gotten "permission" from the head coach to carry on the tradition of shaving the heads of the freshman. Well, I was disappointed. I was hoping that this little tradition might get lost in a season that had suddenly become one of great promises. Upon hearing the "ok" from the head coach I knew what awaited us. After showering and eating dinner in the cafeteria, I headed to town to get a couple of items I had been needing. I returned about an hour later. The football team was housed on the third floor of Webb Hall.

There were not any elevators, and the stairs were located on both sides of the building. About halfway up, I heard my first scream. I paused for a second, but only a second. My thought was really. Screaming? When I arrived on the third floor, I was able to look down the front hallway and there was located the shaving area. Two upperclassmen had the shears, two more had saving lotions and razors.

Suddenly, around the corner there are three upperclassmen dragging a freshman on the floor. The freshman was reaching for anything that he might grab that would slow his journey to a destination that would be final. Standing and watching it all was amazing. After a player had the initial cut from the shears, they mostly resigned to the fact that their precious hair was hitting the floor. When the shaving was completed, they would arise from the chair, shoulders slumped, heads down. Then there was the long trip back to their room, hoping to not encounter a mirror along the way.

I certainly have not always made good decisions, but I did on this occasion. I had witnessed enough of the activity to deduce that resistance would be futile. When I noticed there was an empty seat, I proceeded to walk toward it. I just looked at the guys, sat down, and said, "get it over with". I guess I disappointed them. No screaming, no begging, no holding me down. Whatever it was, after shearing all my hair off, they told me to go on and didn't bother with the razor.

I didn't look in the mirror until the next morning. Of course, I was "horrified" at what I saw. I never had what would be called a great head of hair, but I really did like what I had. I covered it up, best I could, and headed to class. Not only had the upper classmen satisfied themselves with the passing of this wonderful tradition, but they had also made most of the other students on campus smile and laugh as these 20 or so freshman attended class for the first time with their "cue ball" heads.

Reflecting, I should have enjoyed it. In a month the hair was back. It did not hurt anyone and in a lot of ways it did bring the team closer. Two years later this tradition was eliminated.

My mother, Willie Mae, checks
Out my shaves head. Although
Popular today, shaved heads
Were not in style in 1971

Hoops with short shorts

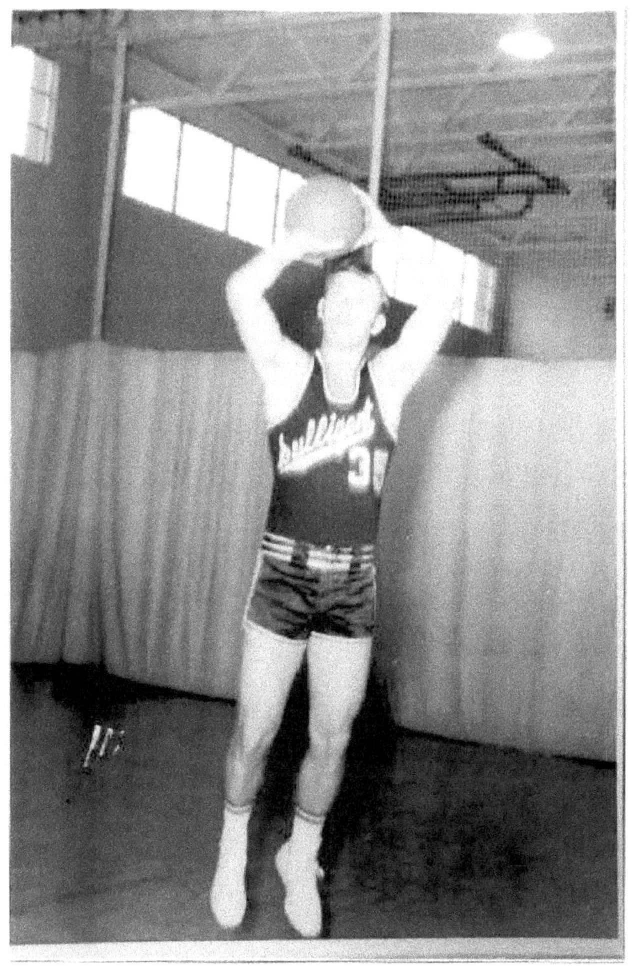

Motivation

After all the physical conditioning, the scheming and strategy, getting the right players in the right positions, no matter what sport, comes the intangible: MOTIVATION.

Does anyone have the ultimate answer to this aspect of athletics? No. However, there have been a lot of tried-and-true methods. I'm not here to talk about them and bore you to death, I'm here to talk to you about the unusual, the weird, and the stranger form of motivation.

Corporal Punishment.

When you hear the term corporal punishment you probably think about paddling for some misbehavior, However, in this instance it was not about misbehavior. It came after several boys had put in a lot of effort on the basketball court and it also came to some that did not even get into the game. In the 1960's Sulligent was having some of its most successful football seasons, especially a stretch from the 1964 season through the 1966 season. They won 28 out of 30 games, losing both of those games to a higher classification school, Fayette High School. They topped it off with a 10-0, AA State Championship in 1966. Larry was the head coach for those last two seasons. However, because Sulligent is a small school every coach was expected to help other sports out. Larry was an assistant basketball coach. Now Larry did not do a lot of coaching during practice, He let the head coach run the program out of respect for that coach's desire to take the program in a certain direction. However, Larry loved to win and was in tense about winning every time he participated in something, He knew basketball well and he knew what the program was about and even better, he knew the basketball players because the majority of them were also football players.

So, one cold, slightly raining, miserable winter's night in the middle of basketball season Larry decided to give his players, what was known at the time as the B-team (today it's often referred to as the JV team), some motivation. However, this motivation was AFTER the game! Besides being a cold, slightly raining, miserable winter's night, the game was also a road contest. It was a game that Larry's team lost. Larry did not blame it on the weather. Larry did not blame it on the referees. Larry blamed it on the players.

As a result, as soon as that game was over, Larry loaded up his players in the cars they had used to travel to the opposing team's town (Busing players to basketball games had not become the norm at the time) and headed back to Sulligent. There was still a Varsity game to be played.

Usually, the B team would be there to support the Varsity players. Not tonight. Larry had decided that his players needed some motivation. Upon arriving back at Sulligent Larry and his players proceeded to the gym. There was not a lot of talking. That had already taken place. The motivation came in the form of corporal punishment. 5 licks with a paddle, to the buttocks to everyone that put on a uniform that night.

No one balked. No one had a self-esteem issue afterwards. No parents called wanting the resignation of Larry. They just went home with a stinging backside and came back the next day ready to practice and get better. I really don't know if it helped, but I'm sure it didn't hurt.

Pass the Paddle

The time is 1966. I am in the eighth grade. This incident occurred during science class. This was not a one-time incident. The teacher for this class was "J. W." His main teaching responsibility was agricultural and welding classes. However, since his degree included a minor in science, he would sometimes be forced to teach seventh and eight grade science. He hated it.

We would often have "free days". A "free day" meant that if all the class would sit quietly at their desks then we would not have any science instruction. The students loved "free days". However, when this incident occurred, J. W. had another plan. He did not want to teach class, but he also did not want to just sit and not do anything. He made an announcement. Today would be "Pass the Paddle" day! The entire class knew what this meant, and it brought much excitement to the room. The rules of pass the paddle were simple. One of the boys would volunteer to take a paddling from J. W. A paddling would be 3 strikes, known in slang as licks, to the behind of the boy. The boy would have to take a stance of leaning forward on a desk. The licks would be administered in such a way as if they were being given as punishment. After the first volunteer took his licks he now "owned" the paddle.

I had never participated in pass the paddle, but I had always intrigued me as to how much power and authority the boy that did have the paddle seemed to possess. The next step was for another boy to volunteer to take a paddling. However, this paddling would not come from J. W., but from the boy that had just received the paddling from J. W. The boy with the paddle did not want a quick volunteer. He had gone through great pain, literally, to gain possession of the paddle and now he would use it to bait some other boy into to taking a paddling from him. When he would challenge another boy, peer pressure would kick in from the entire class, girls included, for that boy to meet the challenge. Sometimes it would work, other times it would not, and he would move on to someone else. Eventually there would be a candidate. When the volunteer received his paddling, the process would start again.

There had been about three volunteers and the class time was about half over when I began thinking. I knew the boy that had the paddle at this moment was not strong or mean. I had never taken a paddling, in fact, I had never had a paddling of any type while in school. I was convinced that this was my moment. As the boy with the paddle scanned the room, throwing out challenges and a few insults, I raised my hand. I would soon have the power. I was an introvert, except for a few close friends, so to volunteer to be paddled in front of the entire class was a socially big step for me. I had convinced myself, "how bad could this be". None of the other boys had cried or acted like much pain was involved. A few had shaken their heads and rubbed their buttocks afterwards, but none had broken down. I was smiling, not cocky, but acting like I was not nervous as I approached the paddling desk. The next few seconds bought excruciating pain to my behind. The paddling kind of took my breath away. After the third lick I paused slightly before turning around. I had to make sure my tear ducts had not opened and was giving my face some time for the color to go back down. Finally, I turned around, with a big smile and said, "is that all you got"? Most of the class was disappointed with my reaction.

Strangely, I did not feel any great "power" while holding the power. I wanted a quick volunteer so that I could paddle him and focus on my pain going away. Shortly, there was a volunteer and I paddled him. In my mind there was not any way that he received the same amount of pain from the paddling that I gave him as compared to the paddling I received. All this time J. W. sat quietly behind his desk, slightly covering his mouth with one hand in an effort to not show his glee. He was having a good day.

That would be the one and only paddling I would receive during my days in school. With corporal punishment being the only real form of punishment, other than calling parents, which in most cases in those days would be worse punishment than what the school would give, a lot of boys would receive several paddling's during the school year. I could not understand why they would rather go through that than follow the rules. Volunteering once during the "pass the paddle" day reinforced my "be on your best behavior during school philosophy".

On The Sideline

In 1978 I had joined my good friends, and former teammates at Livingston University, Ricky Seale and Sam McCorkle, on the coaching staff at Cordova (AL) High School. We stayed together for two years before going our separate ways in our coaching careers. Sam was the head coach. We enjoyed good comradery for several reasons, but the main reason was that we had all played college football under the same philosophy, and we tried to use that experience while coaching together.

We were also good friends and as such often spent time together away from the school and coaching. We would go to college football games because during that time almost every college would give high school coaches free tickets. The requirements for free tickets were the game had to be played on campus and that you were one of the first to call and request the tickets since there was a limited number available. If you were successful, the college that you had called would give you two tickets. You never knew from one year to the next where you would be sitting, and each college would have tickets in different locations. Sometimes you might be I the corner, upper deck, or you might be on the bottom rows behind the players, or you might even have seats around the 40-yard line in the lower section. However, the point was that you were at the game, and you did not have to pay anything to get in.

The following stories all occurred before 9/11/2001. So many things changed after that including the ability to do what we were able to do. After our high school season was over, I started coaching the basketball team. Sam and Ricky were running the off-season program for the football players not on the basketball team. Of course, the college football season still had a few games left and one of the biggest was the Auburn vs. Alabama matchup.

At this time, the Tigers and Tide still played the Iron Bowl in Birmingham. Since this game was not on either one of those schools' campuses there were not any free tickets to be had. However, to the surprise of Ricky and myself, all three of us would be going to the game. Sam told us that he had secured us a way to see the game and to see it for free!

Larry Blakeney was an assistant coach for Auburn. Although I had met him, I would not call him a close friend at the time, but Sam knew him well. Sam was never shy about asking someone for anything. He did not always get what he wanted but he did get a lot of things that most people would not have gotten because they would not have had the courage to ask. Sam had been in a conversation with Larry about how we could get in to see the Iron Bowl. Although Larry would have a certain number of tickets he could give away, he could not waste them on high school coaches but instead needed to give them to boosters. The plan was that we had to be at Legion Field before the Tigers arrived at the stadium. We had to be at the gate which would open to let the buses in that were carrying the players and coaches. Immediately, after the buses had parked, Larry would come to the gate and tell security to let us in. We had to get to the stadium about an hour before the team got there so we would be right by the opening and not have to fight through a crowd to get in.

Step one worked to perfection. We were now inside the stadium. Step two of the plan required us to walk into the playing field at the same time as the players and coaches did. It was a routine for the Tigers, and most other teams, that as soon as they got off the bus, they would walk onto the playing field and do a big circle around it. We mixed in with everyone else and were now on the field of play.

Step two worked to perfection. Step three would be the most challenging. After the players and coaches went into the dressing room it would be an hour before any of them came out to warm up and two hours before kickoff. We would need to blend in with the few reporters, team managers, and others that might be on the sideline, in such a way as to not raise suspicion of security as to why we were there. This was the most nervous time of the whole event. Blending in after the game started would not be a problem. There would be two to three hundred people on the sideline after kickoff and if we did not draw attention to ourselves no one would give us a second look.

Step three worked to perfection, and it was quite the experience being on the sideline for the Iron Bowl. We would move with the reporters from one end of the field to the other as possession of the ball would change from one side of the fifty-yard line to the other. We wanted to stay blended in. Alabama won the game34-16, and since all three of us were Tiger fans, we left disappointed in the outcome of the game but still excited from the whole experience.

We repeated this experience the following year. We were much more comfortable but still at a high level of awareness before kickoff. This game was much more exciting. Alabama entered the game undefeated and ranked number one I the nation. Auburn was 8-2 and were a formable opponent for the Tide. The game was back and forth with Auburn leading with 8 minutes to play in the game before the Tide took the lead. The Tigers would threaten twice more before the game ended with Alabama on top 25-18. Again, we were disappointed in the outcome but enjoyed the experience.

That would be our last college game we would go to together. Sam and Ricky would leave for other jobs while I remained at Cordova for another year. However, that would not be my last sideline experience at the Iron Bowl. I would attend three more and each game would be much different from the others.

In 1981 Bear Bryant was poised to overtake Amos Alonzo Stagg as the winningest FBS coach of all time. Bryant needed 8 wins to pass Stagg and most thought that would happen before the Iron Bowl. However, two upsets had prevented this from happening. A loss to Georgia Tech and a tie with Southern Mississippi meant that if he were going to break the record during the regular season the Tide would have to beat their rival the Tigers. Alabama was somewhat weaker in 1981 after winning back-to-back National Championships I 1978 and 1979 and Auburn, even with a 5-5 record were much better than the year before. They were under the direction of first year coach, Pat Dye, a former assistant under Bryant. The Tigers had lost two games by 3 points and another by 4 and their worst loss was by 14 points.

Larry Blakeney was still at Auburn and since the time I had first met him I had gotten to be more comfortable around him and we knew each other enough that I decided to see if he would repeat the "be at the gate" game experience for me. He said he would be more than happy too. I was no longer at Cordova, but I had a good friend from Cordova who was a huge Alabama fan and I invited him to go with me. As we were traveling to the game, I explained to him all the details of what needed to happen, especially the part about blending in and not showing emotion. I knew this was going to be hard for him to do.

Step one and step two worked to perfection. To make things even better I bought a camera with me and took several photos. I wish I had done this the first two times. The blending in part was much easier since because of the historical importance of the game there were about twice as many reporters on the field than normal, and they were on the field much earlier. We walked in with the Auburn team but drifted over to the crowd of reporters that were surrounding Bryant and ABC announcer Keith Jackson as they walked the field. At times we were within twenty feet of Bryant and Jackson. I took pictures of them along with a picture of my friend and had him take a picture of me on the field.

As both teams eventually went into their respective locker rooms, we started a conversation about what might happen in the next two hours before kickoff. Just as there were many more reporters there was also an increase in security. We did not want to miss seeing the game in person. We wanted so bad to see it from the sideline. The question was to either stay on the sideline or go into the stands. We knew that if we went out of the field and into the stands, we would not be able to get back on the sideline. We also knew that if we went into the stands, we would be guaranteed to see the game. Conservative thinking overtook risk, so we exited the sidelines. We went to the Alabama student section. Student seating is first-come, first-served, which meant your ticket did not assign you to a particular seat. We were able to secure some seats before the section filled up and were now ready to watch the game.

Auburn was leading in the fourth quarter 17-14 but Alabama would score twice to win 28-17 and give Bryant the record for most wins. I do not regret not staying on the sideline because, even though I was wanting Auburn to win, witnessing history being made was cool.

IN 1982 I reunited with my friend Ricky Seale for another sideline experience. However, this one would not be an Iron Bowl and it would not ne I Birmingham but in Auburn. Auburn was hosting Georgia. Bo Jackson was a freshman who was having a season beyond expectations and Herschel Walker was on his way to winning the Heisman Trophy with the Bulldogs. It would be the only college matchup between these two greats.

Although the plan to get into the game was the same as if it were being played I Birmingham, things did not go as well. Ricky and I were at the stadium on time, the team bus drives through, Coach Blakeney comes to let us in, and security says "no". We were shocked, but not as much as Coach Blakeney was. He was already dressed in his Auburn coaching attire, and he had his sideline ID on. He asks again, they say no again. Now he is raising his voice telling them who he is, that we must get inside, and they are still telling him no. Finally, he pauses, and Ricky and I have accepted silently that we are not getting gin to see the game. Finally, Coach Blakeney says one final thing to the security officers, who were an outside firm not affiliated with the university, and they let us in. I do not know what he said to the security officers, and I did not ask. Since he had taken so much time trying to get us in, he did not have time to talk, and we all had to run to make it inside the stadium before all the players and other coaches entered the stadium. Ricky and I went and sat down on an Auburn bench and did not move until the players were on the field.

Auburn led in the fourth quarter but Georgia, who would win the first of three straight SEC titles that year, came back to win 19-14. Jackson had an average day of 58 yards o n13 carries while Walker had 177 yards on 31 carries and surpassed the 5,000-yard mark for his career. It was another great experience seeing the two great running backs on the field as Jackson would go on and later also win the Heisman trophy.

IN 1984, I was back at Legion Field waiting for the Auburn team bus to arrive. I was by myself this time. Everything went smooth and I was again on the sideline waiting for the Iron Bowl. There was little hype for the Iron Bowl I 1984. Auburn was 8-3 and Alabama was 6-4. Auburn was heavily favored to win, but like most Iron Bowls being a favorite is not always a guarantee that you will win. There was not a lot of excitement, in fact it was kind of a boring game. The biggest excitement came from the way Auburn was making too many mistakes and Alabama was playing a solid but not dominating defensive game. In fact, Alabama was leading 17-15 with 3:27 to play. Auburn was at the one-yard line of Alabama. It was fourth down.

As all Alabama and Auburn football fans know, this game is known as "Wrong Way Bo" because Bo Jackson supposedly went the opposite way from which the play was called. However, there were a lot of coaching decisions that contributed to this event. First, Pat Dye admitted that he had not pushed the team to get ready for the Tide and that they had come in flat. Second, Coach Dye elected to pass up the chance to kick a field goal that would have given the Tigers the lead. Thirdly, the play called was not what everyone expected. In stead of getting the ball in the hands of Bo Jackson, the Tigers called a sweep with Brent Fullwood running the ball and Jackson being the blocker. The play was called at the line of scrimmage at the end zone that was made up mostly of Alabama fans, which, according to Jackson, was so loud that he could not hear the play called.

Again, I had my camera with me and got some great shots of the game. I was at about the 15-yard line with my camera up to my eye ready to take a picture of "Bo Over the Top, Part II", but it never happened. In fact, I was so surprised that I did not take a picture of that play at all. In the 1985 media guide there is a full-page picture of this play taken from high in the stadium and you can see me, by myself, holding the camera to my eye as Fullwood is being tackled. Auburn got the ball back and had a chance to win the game with a field goal, but the ball sailed wide left, and Alabama won a major upset.

My last "on the sideline" would be the 1986 Iron Bowl and it would be the most exciting of them all. All the steps to get into the game went smoothly. Both teams came in with only two losses. The game was predicted to be a tossup by most accounts. The main edge was to Alabama in that the game was played on a "neutral field" in Birmingham. There are usually more Tide fans there because Birmingham has traditionally been a strong Tide fan base. The game was exciting even though it was dominated by the defensive play of both teams. Auburn was trailing 17-14 in the fourth quarter, but the real excitement to that point had happened close to the end of the third quarter.

IN all of these "on the sideline" games I never had any type of sideline identification that would prove that I should be allowed on the sideline. None of us had ever been questioned. However, as I was watching the game, I began noticing a police officer eyeballing me. At first, I hoped I was just imagining it, but it did not take long for me to know he was going to approach me. He kept getting closer and closer to me. I guess he was trying to see my armband or some other ID on my body before he asked me about it. Finally, he says, "do you have any sideline ID"? I said, "No sir". He then asks why I am on the sideline instead of immediately escorting me out of the playing area. Up until that moment I did not know how I was going to respond. I then said "Coach Blakeney let me in with the team". Still very suspicious, he says, "why would he do that?" I said, "I am a high school football coach and I have a Blue-Chip prospect that Coach Blakeney is recruiting". Half-truth, half-lie. There is no excuse for lying but I really did not want to miss the end of the game. He says, "show me some identification". I pulled out my drivers license along with my Alabama High School Athletic Association membership card and gave it to him. He looks at them, hands then back to me, and with a still not happy look on his face says, "ok, just stay back out of the way", "Yes sire"!

At 4:54 left in the game, Auburn gets the ball back on their own 33-yard line behind by three points. They start a methodical drive that includes one fourth down conversion. With 32 seconds left in the game, with a second and goal from the Alabama 8-yard line, Lawyer Tillman, Auburn's biggest receiver, is lined up to the right. He does not hear the play call, so he yells at the quarterback for the play. Jeff Burger hollers back at him, "Eighteen Reverse Left". Tillman has never ran this play. It was designed for a different receiver. Tillman tries to call time out but is not given one and barely gets set before the ball is snapped. The Tigers execute the play to perfection and Tillman scores on the reverse. Auburn won 21-17 and it cost Alabama a share of the SEC title.

An interesting footnote is that after the Iron Bowl the Orange Bowl, one of the historically top 4 bowls, invited Auburn to play in its game versus Oklahoma. However, Auburn had already accepted an invitation from the Citrus Bowl to play against USC. Dye would not go back on his word and took the team to Orlando and beat the Trojans 16-7.

Because of 9/11/2001 none of these experiences would be possible today. It is a shame at how much was taken from us on that day.

Herbie Runs Through the Door

As the 1971 football season passed the halfway point things began to slow down for me. After a slow start academically, I was learning the process for being a successful college student. And the tsunami that hit me in the form of college football had subsided and I had gotten used to the expectations, demands, and intensity that was required daily.

It was probably a Tuesday or Wednesday evening when I had stopped to visit two other players in their dorm room. I cannot remember their names, but I am sure they had to be freshmen because I was still intimidated by most upperclassmen. The conversation was not about anything particular but probably contained a lot of discussion about football. A rather boring, but peaceful time of relaxation after what had been a brutal practice (as every weekday practice was) and before going to sleep knowing the same thing was coming the next day. That was before Herbie came through the door. Everyone loved Herbie.

Herbie was a Junior, 6'5" tall, weighing 250 pounds. That is a big man, but in 1971 he was a giant of a football player. He had transferred from the University of Georgia and would become an All American at Livingston as a defensive tackle. Herbie was not in a good mood and the several beers that he had consumed had not helped. He was not mad. Instead, he was sad. He had been fighting with his girlfriend. He started some chit chat with us and, of course, we let him control the conversation. Finally, he started talking about the real reason he was upset. He did not understand women. He never said specifically what had triggered the argument and we never asked. We just listened to him and nodded in agreement with him. As he kept talking about how unappreciative she was and that he was such a good guy to her and how lucky she was to have him, his somber demeaner soon began to change. He was now becoming angry over the situation. We were trying to keep him calm but were not having much success.

Suddenly he stopped talking and his focus was on the door of the dorm room. The doors opened to the inside. You need to know this for what happened next. After several minutes of just looking at the door and being quiet, Herbie says, "Do you all believe I can run through that door?" Our eyes grew big because we immediately knew he was serious. We started telling him that we knew he could, that he could do it easy, that it would not even be a challenge for him. His reply was that he did not think we believed he could. By now his comments were filled with expletives and you could see a physical change coming over him. Deep breaths, intense eyes, and the positioning of his body in an attack position. He kept saying we did not believe him, and we kept saying how much we did. All three of us knew what was about to happen but were holding out hope that it would not.

Suddenly, Herbie explodes toward the door lowering a shoulder and with a loud scream slams into the door knocking it loose from one of its hinges. The door was not completing down, and this only served to infuriate Herbie more, as he quickly backed up and slammed into the door a second time. The door was defeated as it lay helplessly on the floor.

Herbie did not say a word or look back at us. He just slowly made his way down the hall to his room. The door had served as a vessel to release his frustration and he was satisfied.

I slowly, and quietly, made my way back to my dorm room. I never asked those players how they explained a broken door, but I am certain that Herbie was NOT in that explanation. Everyone loved Herbie.

Running the Gauntlet

During my time in high school spring football practice started the second day after basketball season was over, usually the first week of March. It consisted of 20 practices, the last one being an intrasquad game, and all in full pads and full contact. Research what spring practice is like for high schools and colleges these days.

The first day of practice was what most would call a "gut check". It would test your physical and mental capabilities. It was not as hard on me and some of my friends who had been playing basketball because we were in good shape cardiovascular but most of the players had not done anything since the last game in November.

After a short warm up period we immediately began the physical drills. Tackling, one on one contests, three on three contests, and whatever other drills that can be imagined that involved physical contact. After about two hours of this we would line up in an offensive formation, spend about 15 minutes discussing the basics of it, then line up in a defensive formation and spend about 10 minutes talking about responsibilities of each position.

Then a gleam would come over the eyes of the coaches. It was like a kid looking at a shiny new toy on Christmas day. It was time to *run the gauntlet!*

All the players would form a single line file from one end zone to the other. Depending on how many players there were determined the distance from one player to the next. We would usually have around 30 to 35 players on the team. The player at the beginning of the line would then turn around and face all the other players in the line. The coaches would give him a football. It did not matter if you were a lineman or back you would carry the football. The job of the player with the football was to run over the player in front of him. The job of the player facing him was to tackle him to the ground. The player with the ball was not allowed to try and fake the tackler out, he would have to run straight at him. Once the player with the ball was either tackled or had run over the player, he would get up, adjust himself and do the same thing again with the next player in line.

This process would continue until the original player had challenged every other player in the line. It would end after every player had went through the gauntlet. It was a very physical ending to a very physical day. We would all be sore the next day to the point we could hardly move. Day two of spring training would be almost identical to day one but after that it would develop into a more normal football practice.

Nut Job

It is June 1976. I am fresh out of college with my Bachelor of Science degree and have secured a job at Marion County High School in Guin, Alabama. They give me the job of coaching the summer baseball teams. There are four age groups that I am coaching. The tee ball age group, and upper elementary group, and the junior varsity and varsity teams. Most of the practice time is with the younger two groups since a lot of the older players have jobs and other obligations.

The challenge with the tee ball group is that for a lot of them this will be their first experience in an organized setting with little training in the game of baseball. Instruction is needed in the proper way to hit, catch, and throw and which way it is to first base. Most listen to your every word but sometimes a butterfly will come by and attract their attention.

In tee ball a person or player does not throw the ball toward home plate for the batter to hit. An adjustable pole is attached to a rubber, movable plate that sits over home plate. A coach will place a baseball on the end of the pole for the batter to swing at, and hopefully hit. As the coach I would position the player in the batter's box, properly adjust the bat in the hands of the player so he could properly swing at and hit the ball. The last thing I would do would be to place a baseball on the pole for the player to hit.

I would be standing behind the player and would back away from the player a safe distance and tell him to "hit" before he would swing the bat and hit the ball. We had been in season for about two weeks and things were going along smoothly. However, all of that changed at one practice. We would usually do the fielding and throwing drills first and end practice with batting. I was going through the usual steps of batting with a particular player when he swung the bat before I said "hit" which meant I was still within striking distance of his bat. And strike me he did, putting the end of the bat right into my testicles.

OUCH and then some. It seemed that all my breath left my body as I slowly proceeded to the ground immediately curling up in a fetal position. I lay there in agony for a few minutes before I was able to make it to the covered stands where there was some shade. It took a while for things to return to normal and most of the players just stood where they were when it happened. Most did not understand what the problem was. Eventually I was able to finish practice with them, but I was not running any races.

About two weeks later I am conducting practice with the upper elementary group. Most of these players have played a few seasons and have a decent skill level for their age. They all know the rules of the game, so I am trying to teach them the finer points of fielding, throwing, and hitting. We use the same routine as the other age groups and have batting practice last. This age group does have a person throwing the baseball to them. That person was usually me. I am the batting practice pitcher because I can throw strikes and batting practice will go quicker and smoother than having players trying to throw batting practice.

I have a glove and during most practices the players will get 10 swings before their round is up. It is a nice day. Sunny but not hot. Practice is near the end, and I have become a little causal in my approach toward concentrating. I throw a pitch. The batter hits a line drive straight at me. It is not a "hard" line drive, it is just straight at me. With my reactions I have plenty of time to get my glove down and catch it. However, the problem is that I did not use my complete reaction skill and did not get my glove down fast enough to keep the ball from hitting me, yes, in my testicles!

As with the first time, my breath left me, and I slowly went to my knees and then to my side. The difference was that after this age group seen that I was ok most burst into laughter. They knew my pain, but for boys at that age, and above, it is very funny when someone else gets hit in the testicles.

Again, I made my way slowly to the stans and in the shade until I recovered. They were able to continue batting practice without me until I was able to pull myself up, get my eyes straightened out and watch the remaining part of practice.

I played 4 years of little league baseball as catcher and was the starting catcher on the high school baseball team for three years. I coached high school baseball for 25 years. The only times that I ever got hit in the testicles by a baseball was these two times during this two-week period.

Harley-Davidson Homecoming

In July of 2009 I was in Atlanta, Georgia with my daughter and one of her friends for a short vacation before school started in two weeks. While there I received a call from the Superintendent of the Nettleton School District. He was informing me that the current high school principal had received a job offer from another school district and that he wanted to take it. Since he was already under contract for the upcoming school year the superintendent had the power to make him stay. In most situations the superintendent would release him from his contract and let him take the other job. However, since it was only two weeks until the start of the new school year, he had told the principal that he would not release him unless I took his place.

It was a big shock for me. I had spent the previous two years as the assistant principal at the middle school with very few after school responsibilities. This type of lifestyle was very different for me since I had spent the previous 31 years coaching sports. I knew that being a high school principal would bring many more responsibilities and create a much longer work week because of the duties of a high school principal.

I asked the superintendent to give me 24 hours to think about it. The superintendent, Russell Taylor, had worked in the school district for several years, but had only been named superintendent in the spring and was facing his first school year as superintendent. I really liked him as he was a professional and we shared a lot of the same beliefs in how a school system should be operated. I wanted him to be successful and I convinced myself that I needed a new challenge in life. Although I would be receiving a good pay raise, I would actually be making less money per hour worked than I was making as the assistant principal of the middle school.

I gave this background story to lead into the Harley-Davidson homecoming event. Nettleton High School had had 5 principals in the pervious 4 years. Yes, that is not a typo. One of the school years had two retired men serving as principal for one semester each. As you can imagine that had created a culture that fostered discipline issues within the student body and with some of the faculty. There was not any real direction and stability and trust from the office of principal because of the many changes. All the men that served in that capacity during those five years were very competent and professional, but teenagers and adults like, and look, for stability.

There were a few things that after 33 years in education that I knew I had to do to be successful. Gain the trust of both the student body and the faculty, be consistent, be the first one to school everyday and the last one to leave and apply the rules of the school districts handbooks for the students and for the faculty equally to everyone. Although it took me all the first semester, I was able to do gain that trust.

One of the ways to gain the trust of someone is to show them that you have their best interest at heart and that the process is about them and not you. I was constantly looking for ways to accomplish this without compromising the rules of the handbook.

Homecoming is a big deal in the high schools of the South. Since most high schools have football teams, homecoming is usually held on the night of one of the home football games. There is a lot of pageantry during homecoming week. One of the highlights that take place is a parade. The parade usually consists of the police chief leading the procession, followed by a firetruck or two, usually with the cheerleaders riding on them, followed by floats containing the football players and student groups, along with local officials in cars and of course the girls that have been selected by the student body to be maids and homecoming queen candidates.

I was looking for a little different spark for the parade. I decided I would ride my Harley-Davidson Softail Heritage in the parade but would keep it as quiet as possible until the day of the parade. I talked the cheerleader sponsor, who was deathly afraid of motorcycles, to ride on the back. To add an even more elaborate touch to the ride was that I would ride while wearing the school's mascot uniform, a tiger! I positioned myself behind the fire trucks only a few minutes before the parade started but it received immediate attention. Throughout the parade, the students in front of the schools and the adults in town were pointing and laughing and enjoying this extra touch.

I decided to only do this every other year to keep it from becoming routine. Two years later I put on a full football uniform to wear. Only the head football coach, who secured the uniform for me, and myself knew about this one. I left the football field house and drove to the front of the parade just minutes before it was time to start. I circled back around to get behind the firetruck and pointed at my daughter, who was the captain of the cheerleader squad, and motioned her down to get on the motorcycle. It was only when I did that that she realized who I was. All the other cheerleaders laughed with surprise and enjoyed the moment also.

Two years after that I rented a Spider Man costume to ride in the parade. To keep this a surprise, I put the costume on at my house before going to school. Since I lived about five miles from the school, I received several strange looks from other motorists on the highway. The elementary students really enjoyed this costume as I would “spray” spider web at them as the parade passed them by.

The Harley-Davidson homecomings were a big success.

One of the Harley Homecomings.

This one with my daughter, Ashley

Big Dick Butkus

Butkus

From 1965 to 1973 in the NFL fear was spelled B-U-T-K-U-S! Dick Butkus was the middle linebacker for the Chicago Bears. During those nine years he went to the Pro Bowl 8 times, was named first team All Pro 6 times, and was twice named by his peers as the NFL Defensive Player of the Year. Dick Butkus was a fierce, aggressive, and intense player who not only wanted to make the tackle on every play but wanted to inflict pain during the process of that tackle. He was by far my favorite defensive player.

During the 1960's and most of the 1970's NFL teams would play almost every exhibition game in a city that had a large football facility but no NFL team. Birmingham was one such city and my father took me to several games there including the New York Jets v the Houston Oilers in 1966, the New York Jets v the Kansas City Chiefs in 1967 and the New York Jets v the Buffalo Bills featuring Joe Namath and O. J. Simpson, in 1970 to name a few of the games.

In 1968 he took me to Birmingham to see the Baltimore Colts play the Chicago Bears. The biggest name for the Colts was Johnny Unitas and I managed to get his autograph. But the autographed I hungered for was Dick Butkus. I can not remember how I got Unitas' autograph. Probably as he was running on or off the field before or after warmups, but I do remember how I met Butkus as if was happening right now.

In 1968 September 11th was just another day on the calendar that was close to the end of summer. It was a day in between Labor Day and Thanksgiving. It was not anything special. Because of that, rules inside a football stadium were very relaxed. You had to go to your assigned stadium seat but after the first quarter and it was obvious that if there were empty seats closer to the field that no one was coming to use you could move to those seats and the ushers did not care. A person could go to either sideline, either end zone, or just walk around the fence next to the playing field. You could go just about anywhere except you could not exit the stadium and come back in.

It was getting close to kickoff, and I knew if did not get Butkus' autograph before the game started, I would probably not get it. Since we had a long drive back home my father always liked to leave with about 5 minutes left in the game so that we would have a chance to beat the traffic jams that usually occur after a football game.

I decide to be bold. This was not a common trait for me at age 14. I was usually very passive other than on a football field. But this was a different situation. I really wanted the autograph of the greatest linebacker who would play in the NFL.

The locker rooms for both teams were each under the same end zone seats. Access to this area was not restricted, at least not for this game. I started walking toward the locker rooms. I passed the Colt's locker room first and was approaching the Bear's locker room. There had not been anyone standing outside the Colt's locker room but as I came closer to the Bear's I seen two figures. One was dressed in coaching clothes and was dwarfed by the other figure. It was a player that was 6'3" and weighed 250 pounds and had the number 51 on his back. It was Dick Butkus. I assume the coach was the defensive coordinator who was going over last-minute details with Butkus. When I first noticed them, I was probably about 50 feet from them. I paused and then began moving toward them. It did not seem as if I was walking or breathing, just getting closer. When I got within 10 feet of them Butkus slowly turned his head toward me. His facial expression was should I eat you or just let out a giant growl and scare you away. I do not remember if I even asked him if I could have his autograph of if I just handed the program for him to sign. He politely took it, signed his name. and gave it back. I turned away and started breathing again making as straight of a line as I could to find my daddy and tell him what had happened and the success I had had with collecting autographs.

The Colts would beat the Bears 10-0 that night, but to me I was the biggest winner of all!

About autographs, I have never been interested in buying something that has an autograph on it. The only autographs that are special to me are the ones that I see the person sign for me. With today's technology is the autograph on the helmet or football or baseball even real? And if I was not there to see that person, what sentimental value does it hold? I did collect a good bit of autographs over my lifetime, and I will list a few of them besides the ones already mention:

Pete Maravich

Ray Perkins

Scott Hunter

John David Crow

Tony Gonzalez

Ben Davidson

Darryl Larmonica

George Blanda

Brian Piccolo – The subject of the movie “I AM Third” featuring Gale Sayers’

Lou Michaels

Paul Crane

Rico Carty

Ken Stabler

Joe Cribbs

Lynn Swann

Billy Brewer

Marcus Dupree

These a just some of the more recognizable names, but worth looking up if you do not know them.

Friendly, Intense Competition

The events discussed in this section were made possible because there were not any X-Boxes, Nintendo, or other video games available to the youth in the late 60's. I count that as a blessing. With the type of realistic video sports games available today I am not bold enough to say that I would have not become addicted to them like so many youths of today are. Me and my close friends, Carlos Flynn, Mike Knight, and Jimmy Ray loved sports and we each were highly competitive. We all wanted to beat each other in whatever we attempted, but at the end of the day were still friends and never developed any jealousy among us. We all played football, basketball, and baseball and would have attempted other sports if they were available. However, just the organized sports at school would not fill our desire for competition.

We were not pretentious. We did not need attention. None of us had girlfriends until our junior year in high school. We loved to talk about sports. We loved to watch sports, but more than anything else we loved to compete in sports. To get our fix filled in sports we did some unusual things.

On the days that we were not running into home room just in time to beat the tardy bell we needed something to do. Often, we would head to the gym, jerk open the side door, find a basketball, and start playing. Depending on how many of us there were determined the activity we had. If it was three or less, we would most likely play H-O-R-S-E. If there were four or more, we would usually divide into teams and play games. These activities would take place while wearing our clothes that we would wear for the school day. We did not have time to change into gym clothes and back before school started. Of course, the way we played it was not long before we started sweating. This was not a concern for us as we often walked into class soaking. We did not care. We had just had our "energy drink" to get us through the day.

A summer activity, and often on Sunday afternoons, that the four of us would take part in was "wiffle-ball". This was a form of baseball in which a long plastic bat and a plastic, baseball sized ball with holes in it was all the equipment needed. The holes in the ball would make it move in unpredictable ways. You could catch a batted wiffle ball with your hands. The teams were usually Carlos and Mike v. Jimmy and me. Carlos and Jimmy were about the same size and Mike and I were similarly in size. Most of the bases were bushes and home plate could have been anything that was flat. Since it was only a pitcher and one defensive player there were some creative rules.

If a defensive player fielded a ground ball, he could throw the ball to a base and if the ball got there before the runner would be out. The same thing applied if a runner was on base and there was a force out at the next base. Of course, strikeouts and fly balls did not have any new rules, but on the offensive side of the game, if one side got two consecutive hits and that created two runners on base, the lead runner would come in and bat and the second runner would move up to his spot with an imaginary runner taking his spot. These games were a lot of fun, even more so when you run because there was always a sting of defeat in losing.

Competition. Always competing. During basketball season the routine would be as soon as school was adjourned to go to the local restaurant and eat, then to Jimmy's house to kill time before reporting back to school for the game or to travel to another school. Since sitting around was boring. Remember, no mass communication, social media or 24/7 sports channels, we devised our own entertainment, "butter knife hockey"! Jimmy would bring small welding drops, usually about double the size of a BB. That would be the hockey puck. Butter knives would be our stick and plastic cups would be the goals. The carpet floor would be the rink and the goals would only be about a foot apart. Games would be intense as that butter knives/sticks would strike hard and furiously at the puck to go in. Bruised fingers were often the price that was paid in both victory and defeat. After a double elimination tournament, it was usually about time to leave.

After basketball season ended during our senior year in high school, we had four weeks off with nothing to do. Spring training football was in progress. We did not have the means to do much toward the upcoming baseball season except throw to each other and get our arms in shape. We would spend about 30 minutes on this. However, by accident, we discovered something that would make the four weeks fly by. All four of us had went to do something after school one day. We came back to the gym and decided to shoot some basketball. After a bit we decided we needed to play some 2 on 2 games. The usual teams. So, we started playing games that went to "10 buckets". No matter where you were on the court if you scored it was a bucket. You could score all 10 in the paint or from far away, but they all counted the same. We played 5 games that day and would play 5 games every day, other than Fridays during the week until it was time for baseball season. The games during that time turned out to be about a 50-50 draw.

Competition. We loved it.

Guest Speaker

The 1979 football season ended with the Cordova Blue Devils one point away from the State Playoffs. Sam McCorkle was the head coach and Ricky Seales and I were his assistants. However, overall, it had been a successful season. Cordova was full of men who wanted a first-class program and to show their appreciation to the team for their accomplishment the football booster club voted to send us to a bowl game. The club officers along with Coach McCorkle decide that the Peach Bowl in Atlanta would be a good, competitive game and would only be about 3 hours travel time. Sam McCorkle had several different qualities but one of the best was that he was not afraid of asking for anything if he felt that it would help the football program and the players. We could have gotten up early, driven to Atlanta, watched the game, and then came back home. However, he wanted the players to feel like they were special. He talked the booster club into not only paying for a charter bus and the tickets but also into an overnight stay in Atlanta which of course now meant at least two team meals, the evening meal the day of traveling and breakfast the next morning. The booster club agreed.

The two teams in the 1979 Peach Bowl were Baylor and Clemson. Kickoff was 2:30 p.m. Most college football teams arrive at the stadium two hours before kickoff which would be 12:30 for this game. The teams probably had breakfast around 7:30. Afterwards they would have position group meetings and possibly a team meeting and return to their rooms before departing for the stadium. This would be a tight schedule and even through it was a bowl game, both teams wanted one more win for their season.

As I sated before, Sam was not shy about asking for anything if he thought it would help the program. He would often be told "no" but that did not deter him for asking for something else later. About a week before the bowl game, we three were in the football field house talking about different things when Sam says, "Do you think we could get Coach Teaff (Baylor's head coach) to come and speak to the team"? Ricky and my first reaction were "impossible". Then Sam started telling us all the reasons why it was possible and what a great ting it would be. The next thing we know, Sam is calling the football office at Baylor University. When he finally gets online with a person in the department, he starts telling them of his plan. He wanted Coach Teaff to come and speak to the team at breakfast the morning of the game! He leaves a message without any assurances that Coach Teaff will even return his call, much less speak to the team.

Coach Grant Teaff had been hired to coach the Baylor Bears in 1972. He was not their first choice. In a strange occurrence the person Baylor had originally hired stayed one day before resigning! Baylor then hired Coach Teaff. It was the best thing that could have happened to Baylor. Baylor had been 7-43-1 in the five seasons before Teaff's arrival. Three years later the Bears would win the Southwest Conference Championship and he would eventually become the winningest coach in Baylor's history and be elected to the College Football Hall of Fame. Most coaches, particularly head coaches have a game day routine that they never stray from. The odds of getting Coach Teaff to speak to a very small high school football team at breakfast on a game day that had the kickoff set for 2:30 were about as high as winning the lottery. However, those odds did not stop Sam from calling the Baylor football office every day to get an update on his "request". The day we left for Atlanta Sam was told that there was a possibility that Coach Teaff would come speak, but still no guarantee. Sam had given the receptionist the name and location of the hotel that we would be staying at and the time that we would eat breakfast on game day.

We got up early the next morning and Sam was as serious as if he had a game to coach that day. He was waiting to hear if Coach Taeff was actually going to come. About an hour before breakfast Sam got a call. Coach Teaff was coming! We all smiled but Sam paced around the room like we had just gone ahead of our biggest rival in the fourth quarter with only minutes to go in the game. His persistence had paid off. He accomplished something that I did not think was possible.

Coach Taeff arrived just as breakfast had been served to the team. Sam invited him to eat with us, but he declined saying he needed to get back to his team. Coach Taeff gave us about a 20-minute talk about how football can prepare you for life but also about Jesus. Coach Taeff was a Christian and he lived his faith. It was an inspiring speech. Besides being game day for him, with the travel he had to make from his hotel and back and the length of the speech, he also did it for FREE! He did not demand his usual speaking fee but came in hopes of making a difference in the lives of the young men he was speaking to. Football was more than wins and losses to him. This is a story that very few in the vast world of college football know about. There was not any press there, but the Spirit was there and that was what really mattered.

Grant Taeff will always be one of my favorite coaches.

Dabbs and the Relaunch

It was during the summer of 1968 when he walked into my life. At age 15 I did not have a driver's license, so I still depended on my grandfather, Houston Pitts, for transportation. However, on this day I was not needing to go anywhere, I just had rode with him to Sulligent to kill time. Almost every weekday my grandfather would drive to town around 9 a.m. and go to a local grocery store which had a back room in which the local checker players would gather for the daily matches. All these men were very good at checkers including my grandfather. My grandfather did not like to lose. He was very clam except when it came to competition. Card games, dominos, and especially checkers could bring out his temper so much that it would affect his behavior. For the record this behavior did NOT include any verbal or physical abuse but would be things like driving way above the speed limit coming home after a losing match, or just quit playing and shuffle the board, and in one case leaving town and going home without my grandmother who had gone to town with him on that day!

On the days that I would travel to town with him I would usually just walk around the block several times, go into some of the stores, there was one area that had covered stairs I would venture up, and sometimes I would walk to the school which was about a quarter of a mile from the stores part of town. There was not a lot to do there but it there were some swings and other playground equipment that would help pass the time.

I was sitting on a large tree stump when a man walked up behind me and after saying some type of greeting wanted to know my name and said his was Dabbs Earnest. He said that he would be an assistant football coach but more importantly the new head basketball coach. He wanted to know if I played either. I told him, both. We carried on a conversation about both sports and what positions I played and how long I had been playing. After a while the subject of baseball came up. He wanted to know if I liked baseball. YES, was my reply. He wanted to know how long it had been since Sulligent had a baseball team. I told him 3 years. He asked if there would be enough other boys who would want to play for him to determine if we could have a program the following spring. I assured him there was.

I was excited for a few days after our meeting, but that died down as football practice started. The football season was a big disappointment as Sulligent had its first losing season in several years. It would be the only losing season as a player that I would experience. I did not like it. On the first day of basketball practice, the Monday after the Friday finale, all the basketball players were waiting in a small room for our first meeting as a team. Coach Earnest was not there yet. We all knew that Coach Earnest was a serious man particularly about sports, but we really did not know the full extent of his seriousness. Suddenly, the door open and in walked Coach Earnest. He was a little late because he had left school and went to get a haircut, a "flat top"! Since his arrival in the summer, he had wavey hair, not long, but not short, but no one had "flat tops" at that time.

There were almost a few snickers, but they quickly subsided when we seen the fire in his eyes. Silence came across the room without him having to say a word. He went directly into what his philosophy of basketball was, his expectations of us, and the dedication he would be requiring. Coach Earnest was a stern but fair coach. He had already gained the respect of the entire student body in only a few short months. He brought great excitement among the players, school, and community about the basketball program. He absolutely knew what he was doing. He was such a humble man that it would be almost two years after his arrival that we found out that he had been a college All-American in both basketball and baseball!

We had a great season and as soon as it was over, he had a meeting with everyone that was interested in playing baseball. This was very exciting for all of us who had missed playing and loved baseball. He told us that we would have a team. Great! Everyone was wondering the obvious. We did not have field. The new gym was built on the infield of the old field. His answer was that we would be playing every game on the road. A little shocked, but that quickly subsided. Anything to get on the diamond again.

After a few days of practice in literally a field with all kinds of different grasses and weeds with nothing other than some baseballs and a couple of bats we were going to get our uniforms. First, he gave us our pants, leggings, and hats. Then he gave us our tops – FOOTBALL JERSEYS! There was a little bit of smiles and a few jokes but not any real complaints. We were not so vain that we would give up a baseball season just because we had to wear football jerseys.

In the spring of 1969, we played 14 games on the road going 6-8. Everyone could tell that we had not played baseball in a while, but we all could see the potential we had. We played some summer league games. In the spring of 1970, we played 15 games on the road, going 10-5, winning the area championship, and one game in the state playoffs before our season ended. We were proud even with our football jersey tops. You could see the disappointment in the eyes of our opponents when shaking hands after a game when they had a lost. The disappointment came from losing the game but was compounded by the fact that they had just lost to a team wearing football jerseys.

About a month before the 1970 season started, construction began on a new baseball field. The town of Sulligent was building it. It would have dugouts, a press box, lights tall enough to give out good lighting. And most importantly an outfield fence to go along with the side fences. The reason this was important was that a lot of schools during that era did not have outfield fences, but now we did!

The new "stadium" was built in time for us to play some summer games on it. The next spring, 1971, led by six seniors, including myself, we would play home games, we would go 16-2, we would win the West Alabama Conference championship and we would reach the AA State Championship series were our only two losses of the season would come. And we did it also with true baseball tops. No more football jerseys. We were never ashamed of wearing football jerseys, but it was nice having a complete baseball uniform.

Dabba Earnest did not have to go to all the extra trouble for Sulligent to have a baseball team. He was hired to be the basketball coach. However, he loved young people and coaching was a calling for him. I will forever, be grateful for him relaunching the baseball program at Sulligent.

AREA CHAMPS
3rd Row: JAMES WINSTON, LARRY TURNER, BILLY MADDOX, LEMUEL BOYETTE, COACH EARNEST
2nd Row: MIKE NOLEN, CARLOS FLYNN, MIKE KNIGHT, GARY SORRELS, MITCHELL STONE, JIMMY RAY
1st Row: DANNY HOLLIS, ODIS HESTER, JERRY PITTS, KENNETH HUMBERS, LARRY NORTHINGTON, DALE KNIGHT
1970 10-5

Chapter 2

Injuries

Y. A. Tittle, the New York Giants quarterback, was injured late in a game which the Giants lost. This was in 1964 and it inspired me to accept the fact that football players must play with pain, and sometimes injury.

Injuries

If a person decides to play football, remember, football is a voluntary activity, then he must accept the fact that pain will be involved. This pain may be just sore muscles from normal football movement activities, it may be from the contact involved in football that may leave bruises or swelling, it may be from jammed fingers, scratches, or slightly pulled muscles. Football players, most of them, will have some type of pain the entire season. They will practice with this pain, and they will play with this pain. A person who cannot deal with pain of this type will not play football very long. That is one of the reasons that football is NOT for everybody and it also one of the reasons that it is so popular. Spectators like to watch football players knowing that most are playing in pain. Again, if you have never played football, or if you have and the pain drove you away from it, do not try to change the game to reduce the pain players experience. FOOTBALL IS A VOLUNTARY ACTIVITY AND NO ONE IS BEING FORCED TO PLAY. PEOPLE PLAYING FOOTBALL KNOW THAT THERE ARE RISKS INVOLVED.

Injuries are different. A good, experienced, dedicated player will know the difference between pain and injury. Some examples of injuries that would keep someone from practicing or playing would be a concussion, a complete break in the arm of leg, a torn muscle, ACL tears and other knee issues, or other internal injuries. However, there have been a lot of examples of were players participated with broken hands or fingers, slightly broken arms or legs or slightly torn muscles. These players play because they have a different toleration of pain, a dedication to the team, and desire to play for individual reasons, that are much greater than the average football player. They should not be condemned for playing with these conditions. They should not be used as examples to force other players to do the same. It is an individual decision and should stay that way.

The first 'injury" that I *thought* I had was a pair of swollen hands. I was in the eighth grade and practicing with the varsity team while playing on the junior high team. I asked my daddy if I could go to the doctor and let him evaluate them. He said OK and I checked out of school and walked about four blocks to where the clinic was located. Once I was in the examination room and the doctor came in to look at the hands, which were both smooth because of the swelling, he asked me one question. "Do you play football?" My answer was "yes". All he then said was, "you are ok, go back to practice this afternoon", and then left the room. Everyone in the community looked up and admired this doctor, so I did not have a second thought about his answer. I was back at practice that afternoon. A lot of kids today would be out a week or so with that type of "injury". I am glad he set the tone for me to develop a mindset of playing with pain because it would be helpful in the future.

There was one day left in my junior season of high school. We were 5-4 and were slight favorites in our final game against Carbon Hill. It was a Wednesday and we had had a relatively mild, but still in full pads, three days of practice. Thursday's practice would be in shorts and helmets and last about 30 minutes. We already had two key players, including 6'5" 220-pound running back Randy Johnson out for the game with injuries and did not need any more. The last thing, and only time during the week, on Wednesdays, we would go over all the aspects of the kicking game. Kickoff coverage, kickoff return, PAT and field goal attempts and blocks, punt coverage, punt return, and the last thing punt block. Punt block would be the last single practice activity of the 1969 season. Thursday would only be going over who was were on the different special teams, running a few offensive plays and lining up in the defensive formations. We had executed the punt block scheme twice. We did not even have live blocking. My technique was to go through the center and guard gap which would hopefully be opened by a defensive player on each of them and pulling them sideways to give me a clean opening. My head coach said, "one last time." He wanted us to execute the punt block scheme one last time before ending practice. As I ran through the gap and jumped in the air everything was a normal as all the other times that I had done it during the season. When I came down is when everything changed.

It was in the most excruciating, agonizing, intense pain of my life. I had turned my left ankle. It swelled immediately. There was a bulge the side of a golf ball on the outside of my ankle. I could not hold in the yells. Coach Elliott sent the team to the field house while a couple of players helped me to it. They had one "instant ice" pack which they used on it. They called my daddy. He came and got me and took me to the doctor. He gave me some aspirin, said there was not much he could do for it, then gave me some crutches, and said to stay off it as much as possible. I went to school the next day, but I did not play that night. Besides playing center and linebacker I was also the snapper for punts and PAT's. The replacement punter snapped one over the punter's head which set the Bulldogs up in great field position and they took advantage of it by scoring a touchdown. The final score was Carbon Hill 22, Sulligent 14.

Looking back, if the coaches and doctor, and even myself had known how to treat ankle injuries as well as those same people know today, I might have played. At least I might have been able to long snap. If I had started rotating ice baths for it, 15 minutes in ice, an hour out, 15 minutes in ice, etc. If I had kept it elevated other than during the ice baths instead of going to school the next day, if I had taken stronger inflammatory medicine, if I had taken a shot of Novocain, and with a good taping of the ankle, I might have been able to play, at least have been able to long snap.

I was very disappointed. It would be the only game, football, high school and college, basketball, and baseball, of my career that I would miss because of injury. However, it did not mean that I was never injured again.

In January of 1973 I had returned to Livingston. There had been a change in head coaches. Jim King, an assistant, was promoted to the head coach of the Tigers after Mickey Andrews had left for Florence State (University of North Alabama now). I was ready to return to playing football. I called a couple of SEC schools and they told me at the time, even through I had sat out a year, under NCAA rules I would have to sit out another season to be eligible. That would not work. I contemplated about staying at Florence State, which I was now attending as a regular student. I had talked to my father about returning to football. When he returned home from work one day, he told me he had been working behind the scenes to get me back on the team at Livingston. He had called Clemit Spruiell, who had played at Sulligent and who was the quarterback of the Tigers 1971 National Championship team and had discussed what I was wanting to do. Clemit was now a graduate assistant at LU. My father said that Clemit would be calling later that night with Coach King in the room. I had to convince them I was ready and wanting to play. Around 7 p.m. we get a call from Clemit. He starts asking me some questions. We did not know Coach King was listening to the conversation. After a bit Clemit put me on the phone to talk with Coach King. Evidently, my father's conversations with Clemit had already set the groundwork for my return contingent on how I answered the questions during the phone call. Coach King eventually welcomed me back with a full scholarship but with one stipulation, I had to be in Livingston the next morning by 7:30 a.m. Livingston University was on the quarter system at that time which meant they started earlier than schools on a semester system and all major classes met five days a week. Clemit and Coach King had already done the leg work to schedule the classes that I would need that quarter and the next to be eligible to play in the fall. I was on time and thankful to be there. I was also very thankful to my father and Clemit for the effort they had put into my return, but very thankful to Coach King For giving me a second chance, when he could have easily written me off as a quitter.

I went through off-season workouts, spring training, and headed home for the summer. I had lost a lot of my technique after being away from football for a year. I was working hard but my skillset was slow in coming back. Upon returning to campus for the beginning of fall workouts before the season started, I knew that I had used up all my chances. I knew that I must perform well enough to keep my scholarship and hopefully get to play some.

I can not imagine another place hotter and more humid in August than the campus of Livingston University. For some reason it seemed to cool off some once the season began but for those four weeks leading up to the first game it was brutal. Individual technique drills were a daily occurrence. One of the drills involved was a tackling drill in which the defensive player tackled the running back at an angle. The technique for the defensive player involved putting the side of the helmet across the chest of the running back, locking up with both arms. Running a few steps, and then bringing the running back to the ground. It was a drill that was used in nearly every high school and college at that time and one that I had done many times.

During the second week of practice, we were doing this tackling drill. When I did it, I did everything perfectly but as I came to the ground my shoulder pad flap protecting my right shoulder came up enough that I landed directly on my AC joint. During our fall the running back was on top of me, and this added extra force to the unprotected joint. I was hurting. I held my voice, but I knew something was wrong. I got back in line, without saying a word, and eventually did the drill again. Most football players use their shoulders to some extent no matter what position they play. However, as a linebacker I was using mine on every snap. It did not matter if it was trying to knock down offensive linemen or to tackle a running back, my shoulders would be impacted every running play. I could not tell the coaches. I was afraid of what they might find. I knew I could not miss any more time. As the season went on, I finally earned a starting position in the 7th game of the season. I would start every game from then on while at Livingston. My shoulder was continually getting worse. At outside linebacker I would line up on the tight end no matter which side he was on. My first assignment was to deliver a blow to the tight end to slow him down from his blocking assignment or his ability to release for a pass. During that era most teams would have their tight ends line up on the right side of the formation which meant I would be using my right arm to deliver a blow to him on every play. Occasionally the tight end would line up on the left side and I would use my left arm. But that was very rare.

Now that I was a starter on the defense, I certainly was not going to tell the coaches about my injury. I was just going to have to play with the pain. I did have one option that I used. Without telling anyone, including my father, who did not know about the injury, I skipped classes one morning, drove to Sulligent, and visited my lifelong doctor. The same one that sent me to practice with swollen hands. I told him about the injury, how it happened, and what my status was with the team. I told him I could not miss any more time. He understood, left the office, and came back with the biggest needle I had ever seen. It was filled with cortisone. He placed the needle in my AC joint and gave me probably the biggest dose that he was allowed to give. Within a few minutes I was feeling much better. I headed back to Livingston and practiced that afternoon. Again, I did not tell my coaches. I got this shot with two games to go in the season and it helped tremendously. I made this trip twice more, once during off-season workouts and once during spring training. Finally, out of curiosity my doctor called Coach King. He asked him if he knew that I was injured and that I was driving to Sulligent to get the cortisone shots? Of course, Coach King did not. As we were getting dressed for another spring training practice Coach King called for me in his office. He asked me if what the doctor said was true. I told him it was and my reasons for it. He was a bit shocked. After asking how I felt, he said anytime you need to miss practice to go get a shot just let us know. I felt relieved. The coaches now knew about my injury, how I had played through the pain, and I had also earned a starting position with the knowledge that if I needed to miss a day or two of practice no other player would be put ahead of me.

By the time the 1874 season I was in the best shape of my life. I was also playing the best football of my life. I would be named the Tiger Defensive Player of the Year and to the first team all Gulf South Conference defensive team. We were having a great season at 7-1 until we lost two of our last three games to finish at 8-3. I had gotten two more shots but was prepared to have a surgeon fix it.

At that time Livingston University was using Hughston Orthopedic Clinic in Columbus, Georgia for any of their athletes that needed surgery. I had not been officially told I needed surgery, but I was confident that I did. After visiting the clinic, taking X-rays (There were not any MRIs at that time and that would lead to a big surprise later), and doing some hands-on examination the physician determined that I did indeed need surgery. It was scheduled for two weeks later.

The physician who would perform the surgery was Dr. James Andrews. This is the Dr. Andrews who would become famous worldwide for his capabilities concerning joint injuries. He would operate on NFL. NBA, and Major League baseball players. He would operate on college football players from Division II schools to SEC schools. He was the official team doctor for Livingston and Auburn University at the same time. He would operate on famous golf players and soccer stars, but he would also operate on people who had never been an athlete but had joint issues He was an extremely intelligent and compassionate doctor and one that made you feel like you were the only patient that he had. However, in 1974 he was just getting started.

A Tiger basketball player, who needed knee surgery, would be accompanying me to Columbus. I was in a pretty good mood because I knew that having surgery would get out of the extremely physical and mental demanding off-season workouts. I slept well the night before surgery and had a ho-hum attitude about it early the next day when the nurses came to get us. If I only knew what was about to happen.

I had never had an operation and only knew one person, my mother, that did. She had been in a lot of pain afterwards, but I could not relate to it. I assumed it would be like a headache and would last a couple of days.

I woke up screaming! The anesthesia had worn off and it was not time for pain medicine. I thought that my arm had been cut off and I struggled to see if it was there. My roommate, the basketball player was also screaming in pain. He knew that he was going to get his anterior cruciate ligament (ACL) repaired, but after they cut him open, they had to also repair his posterior cruciate ligament (PCL) and Medial Collateral ligament (MCL). His basketball career was over. About 30 minutes after they bought us back from surgery, we were given some pain medicine, morphine. We calmed down and slept for about two hours before the doctors came in to talk to us. Dr. Hughston had down the basketball player's surgery and Dr. Andrews had done mine. Dr. Andrews first words to me was, "You liked to have waited too long." Because MRIs had not been invented and X-rays were the main thing for doctors to use to see what was going on inside the body, surprises would sometimes await them. In my case Dr. Andrews knew I had an AC joint separation with a possible tear of one of the ligaments or tendons. When he cut me open all 4 main ligaments were torn, the four major tendons were torn, there was some muscle torn, and some bone chips floating in it. When He performed surgery on that shoulder for the third time, placing in an artificial shoulder, 36 years later, he told me that that was still the worse shoulder he had ever seen.

Since everything was torn and, in a mess, he did not have the option of using tendons or ligaments that had not been torn as a basis for repair. In a rare procedure he cut my Pectoralis Major to the inside and stretched it across my shoulder and stapled it to the backside of my shoulder. He then was able to repair all the ligaments and tendons. He cleaned out the bone chips and repaired the muscle as best he could. He literally saved my arm.

I had played 15 games, went through and off season and a spring training with this injury. I don't know how much was torn on the initial injury and if I knew that it was that bad, I probably would have said something. I am forever thankful to Dr. Andrews.

Besides the previous mentioned awards that season I was also given The Most Dedicated Award.

Nothing can top that on my personal list of injuries, but I did have a few more and some issues later in life that were probably related to playing football.

In no particular order of injuries, they are:

Right shoulder, operated on 3X, the last one a shoulder replacement was performed.

Back surgery on L5, 2X. I originally hurt my back in the 8th game of my Senior season.

Both wrists operated on.

A bruised sternum that I played with my Junior and Senior years in college. One of the most painful injuries that does not hurt unless it is hit and then it will bring you to your knees. I used a special pad to protect it.

Neck surgery 2x. C4 and C6 the first time and C5 the second time.

A broken left hand (against Troy State my Senior year. The trainer padded it up and I continued playing.)

A hyperextended elbow

A turned ankle

Left hip replacement

Some of the injuries bother me some today, most do not. However, I want to make one thing clear. I would never give up what I gained by playing football regardless of what my body experienced then or now. I had rather live like a lion for 50 years (more than that now, lol) than live like a lamb for 100 years.

Chapter 3

It Had Its Affect

A lifetime in athletics led me to cross paths with many other people in athletics. Brandon Rea, an assistant football coach at Nettleton (MS) High School, and myself,

It Had Its Effect

When one looks back over their life, they can often easily look at events that were unique, important, positive, negative, or sometimes just a "come on man" situation. Below are several of these events. They are not in any order but all worthy of writing about.

First Football: When I was around 8 years old, I was outside my housing, playing as usual, when a cousin of mine, on my daddy's side, much older than me stopped by our house on her way home after work. She got out of her car and gave me a new football! To the best of my memory that was the first football that I had ever had. I was speechless and could hardly say thank you. I wore that football out. I was not expecting anything from her. We were not real close, but she was close with my daddy. It instilled in me that sometimes the best time to give is when someone is least expecting it.

Nfl Punt, Pass, And Kick Contest: In 1961 the Ford Motor Company and the NFL started what was known as the Punt, Pass and Kick contest. It was designed for pro football which, believe it or not, was not a nationwide sport of popularity, particularly compared to day's popularity, in a way to increase interest from youth football players. It was a simple contest. A participant would punt, pass, and placekick a football. The distances would be totaled, and the highest total would win. There were different age groups so that it would be fair. I never won but I did receive a booklet with the NFL logo on it and that meant a lot to me.

Electric Football Game: I am certainly glad that X-box and all the other highly technical video games and game systems were not available when I was a youngster. I am sure I would have been as addicted to them as youngsters are today. I would not have been outside developing my athletic skills, or riding bicycles for miles each day, or climbing trees. However, I was blessed to have one of the first electric football games. This game was a piece of rectangle metal in the shape of a football field. It had all the markings of a field and goal posts. It was elevated about two inches. It came with two teams of plastic players. Some of the players were in linemen positions and some were in what would be consider running back or receiver positions. The feet of each player went into a square and on the bottom of each square was two, very thin, pieces of firm plastic. The board had a device underneath it so that when the current was turned on it would slightly vibrate which would cause the players to move. People playing the game would set up their players in both an offensive and defensive formation. One player on offense would have a tiny cotton football. Once both formations had been set someone would turn the board on and it would stay vibrating until either a defensive player touched the offensive player that had the football, or the offensive player scored. It was a lot of fun. Much slower than a video game and not enough fun to keep me inside more than I was outside. I enjoyed those as a kid and was blessed with one when my wife Leslie found one on the web and surprised me with it one Christmas. I do not play it but have it set up and look upon it with fond memories of my youth.

Breakfast Of Champions: My mother and father were member of the "Greatest Generation" and were salt of the earth type of people. Yes, they had their faults like we all do, but being slackers was not one of them. I had an unique breakfast during the school year for the entire time I was in elementary and secondary school. My mother had a job in factory that made clothes. They were called "garment plants". It was hard work for little pay, and they had to meet a quota to receive their minimum wage. Every morning before work, which started at 7 a.m., my mother would make home-made, from scratch, biscuits. Not the ones in a can, but by using flour and milk and whatever else it takes to make them. They would be huge. I would then take two, open them in the middle and spread them on my plate. The next step was to pour coffee slightly over them, not enough to make them soggy, but enough for taste. I then topped the with some sugar and had the "breakfast of champions".

SKILLS DEVELOPMENT: I was almost seven years old before my parents had my sister. The age difference, and with her being a girl, kept was from being close growing up. I was totally interested in sports, particularly football and baseball. I wanted to play and be the best I could be but the only organized sport growing up before junior high school was little league baseball and that usually consisted of about 12 games during the summer. Fortunately, we had a big yard, in the country, that gave me the opportunity for movement. Some of my athletic skill was natural as both my grandfather and father were good athletes. They had not excelled in sports because of the demands that life put on them to make a living, but you do not have to pay sports to be an athlete. My father played high school football until he dropped out of school at age 17, joined the Navy, and was sent to the Pacific theater during World War II. Riding a bicycle for miles/hours during some days helped my coordination, speed, and lower body strength. There were not any gears to the bicycles I rode, but there were lots of hills. Climbing trees helped my upper body development, mental judgement, and coordination. When I say climbing trees, I mean sometimes going up 15-20 feet, out on branches, and fortunately, never falling. I developed specific skills in baseball by throwing a rubber ball against the chimney. I would play imaginary games by pitching to batters. Sometimes they would hit the ball, sometimes they would swing and miss, sometimes they would walk. However, whatever happened I was developing my throwing motion and arm strength with each pitch. At times I would throw the ball at an angle that I would have to go far to my right for a backhand catch of the bouncing ball or far to my left for an open hand catch of the ball. Sometimes I would just sit on the carport and one bounce the ball against the house back to myself. Right-handed, then left-handed. We had a circular driveway to the side of the house, and it was about 90-100 feet on each side. The county road separated our property from a bank that was about 20 foot high. On top of the bank was trees and underbrush. The bank was about 180 feet from the furthermost part of the circular drive. All we had were wooden bats during those times. Wooden bats were perfect for hitting rocks. Rocks were perfect "baseballs". This setup was even better for the imaginary games than the chimney. I would pick out a "baseball" and hit it. Sometimes it would be a ground ball out, sometimes a single, sometimes a fly ball out, but if the rock hit the bank it was a ground rule double and if it landed on top of the bank it was a home run. I batted for both teams, but usually my team found a way to win. I wore two bats completely in to over several summers playing these games. It was a tremendous help to my eye and hand coordination and developed my wrists and forearms. My daddy also bought a table tennis for me when I got older. We really didn't have enough space to play one properly, but we did have enough room to get the skills for quick reaction and eye and hand coordination out of playing it as it was very popular with my friends.

Developing football skills by oneself is much harder than other sports. However, with my football I would also have imaginary football games. These games would consist of passing plays, tackling, and being tackled, punting, and covering punts, and being "injured" only to come back and continue. I guess the best thing I got out of these games was a mental outlook as to how the game of football should be played.

EARLY COMPETITION: Entering the eight grade of school I was beginning my third year of organized football. I had played on the junior high team during both my 6th grade and 7th grade school years. However, as an eight grader, I would now be practicing with the varsity players daily. This would be a turning point in my life as both a football player and lessons learned to help my maturity. This varsity team was so good that I played in every game but one, a couple of games I played in the first half. They would be so ahead of the other teams that Coach Yancy would start substituting early in the game so to not run up the score. I even had an interception in a varsity game as an eight grader. The real difference and benefits I got from this season were what happened at practice and the positive events that took place. The 1966 Sulligent Blue Devils were the state class AA champions.

REBEL: I know this will sound ridiculous in today's world, but I did a couple of things that was "rebellious" during my high school days. My daddy was wise beyond his education. We had very few disagreements, however, looking back almost all his actions helped me. Entering the seventh grade I had a full head of hair with bangs down to my eyebrows. One Saturday morning, my father says, "let's go to town, you are getting a haircut". Well, I did not think I needed a haircut, but I was guessing a little trim on the side would not hurt anything. A little trim was NOT what my father had in mind. As we approached the barber shop, he proceeded to tell me "you are getting a crew cut" a "crew cut" is a politically correct way of saying you are getting all your hair cut. I knew he was serious, and I knew there was little chance of a compromise. I did manage to get him agree to having a small flap of hair in the front that came down about three inches. I guess his thinking was that hair would lead me to girls, which would lead me away from athletics. Probably some truth in that. I had that hairstyle for four years. Before my junior year I sheepishly ask my father if I could grow my hair out. Surprisingly, without any lecture or comment, he said, "ok". I let my hair grow out and with it I also let my sideburns grow. They eventually grew to an inch or so below my earlobe. Another battle was brewing. My daddy did not like them, and my basketball coach did not like them. There were a couple of heart-to-heart conversations about them at the time. Joe Namath was my favorite football player at the time. Broadway Joe had the long sideburns. To my father this equaled me to eventually having the same off the field lifestyle that Joe lead. Of course, it never happened, and I kept the sideburns.

"MANDATORY VOLUNTEER" WORKOUTS: Because of our success in football my Senior year the season pushed way into basketball season. Coach Earnest was 100% wanting us to win in football, but his love was basketball. The day after our defeat in the semi-finals of the state playoffs we were in the gym for "voluntary" workouts. Just shooting and a few drills. Not any conditioning. That would come Monday. We had a basketball game that Tuesday and we had enough talent that against a weaker opponent we easily beat with only one day of official practice. Friday of that first week we played Hamilton. A powerhouse for sports in our area the Aggies had been practicing and playing basketball games for about three weeks. We got beat pretty bad. What happened after the game has remained a mystery to this day. In the locker room Coach Earnest is going crazy. Something he rarely did. We all knew that when he said anything, he meant it and rarely did he raise his voice. The topic of conversation did not involve us as players, not hustling, making too many mistakes, being intimidated, or anything to go with what had went on the court. He was saying we went focused and had been looking up in the stands at our girlfriends! He immediately banned us from our girlfriends. He was nice enough to say that we could take them home this night and tell them the "good news". The "ban" meant no public contact with them for the remainder of the basketball season. No bringing them to home games or taking them home after any games. No walking beside them in the hallway or sitting close to them in class at school. No dates in town. Nothing. And we knew he meant it. He did not tell us what the consequences of breaking this ban would be, but you did not have to be a genius to figure it out. If he caught you the first time it would probably have meant running you until you felt like you were going to die. A second violation would have been removal from the team. Did we adhere to this rule? We did about 90% of the time. There were times that we went to other towns with our girlfriends and a couple times they met us away for school and rode home with us after games. Three of us players almost got once when we drove past him with our girlfriends in the car. Fortunately, he did not notice us. All the players swore to him, and each other, that no one was looking in the stands at their girlfriends. I had not been looking and I do not have any reason to believe that any other player had. After a few years of being a coach myself I wanted to ask him about this situation. He passed at an early age and I did not have the opportunity to talk with him about it. I believe, after years of being in a college program and then being around different coaches after I became one, is that his actions were just a ruse to make sue we were focused on the basketball season. We were late getting started. We had a great football season and people were still telling us how great it was. Nine of the first 10 players had been on the football team. He knew he had to get our attention on the basketball season, immediately, or it would be quickly over and unsuccessful. He could have talked to us about it and pleaded with us to put football behind and make basketball the main thing. Kind of like how coaches do these days, or he could blast us with this accusation of treason and demand totally loyalty or else! It worked.

HUMILATION: One of the characteristics of Coach Earnest that helped me as a person, player, teacher, and coach was that no one received special treatment because of who they were, who their parents were or their athletic ability. There were several instances in which I witnessed him putting this philosophy in practice on students and athletes. I had escaped this wrath for nearly three years since he had come to Sulligent. However, in the spring of my Senior year it was my turn. The school was having an assembly for a talent show. It was the usual talent that is displayed at these events with music being the dominating factor. The highlights were by a local band that had recent graduates and current students in it and by an unplanned event. Another Senior, Billy Maddox, was the leader of the band. They put on a great performance by having the band members, starting with the drummer, come out one at a time. The drummer started the song, and each additional member would pick up their part until finally Billy came out and began the lyrics. The song was "Gimmie Shelter" by the Rolling Stones. Billy did not dance around like Mick did when performing but he did a fantastic job with vocals. Most of the students thought that the assembly was concluded but Coach Earnest had one more trick up his sleeve. During basketball season the players had to stay away from their girlfriends during the school week. No one had gotten into any trouble over this even though we had not abided by it 100%. Since this assembly was several weeks after basketball season what was about to happen surprised everyone. Coach Earnest had been the Emcee of the assembly and when he came to the microphone everyone thought he was going to instruct us on how to proceed with the rest of the school day. That was not the case. I do not remember exactly how he started, but I became more focused on his words as he continued. When it got to the part that "a certain player has broken a team rule about being with their girlfriend during the basketball season" he had my full attention. Further explanation on his part gave a though understanding to the student body. He then announced the guilty party – "Jerry Pitts". Well, I was in shock and I was also sitting with my girlfriend which was not off limits by that time. He instructed me to come down to the gym floor. Since the entire student body was in the gym, students were sitting shoulder to shoulder and that resulted in me taking a while to get to the floor. All eyes seemed to be on me and no one, including myself, knew what to expect. At this point Coach Earnest was having more than a little fun at my expense. He was talking about the "crime" and the "punishment". He reached into his pocket and pulled out a shiny penny. "Pitts, in order to absolve yourself of this crime, you must put this penny on the floor and push it to the other end using only your nose!" A moment of silence was followed by outrageous laughter. I paused for a moment and then knew what I had to do. I got down on all fours and began to push the penny with my nose. It was difficult at first and I was not making much progress. However, about a third of the way I was beginning to get the hang of it and was able to move the penny about four to five feet with each nose push. The student body was enjoying this immensely and especially the guys I hung out with as it was natural for all of us to give each other a hard time about anything any chance we had. After completing the length of the court, I picked up the penny and held it high like I had just completed an Olympic event. I was smiling, Coach Earnest was smiling, and I am sure 99% of everyone watching was smiling. I never asked him if had really caught me breaking the rule or if he just decided to have some fun at my expense. I did not need therapy afterwards. It just gave me more respect for a man that I already had great respect for.

GOING FORWARD, BACKWARDS: After five grueling, eye opening, physically demanding, mentally exhausting weeks of preseason practice during my freshman year at Livingston University it was finally game time! The first game was against Jacksonville State University, but it was being played at Anniston, Alabama instead of Jacksonville. I had made the travel squad and was going to start on the kickoff coverage team. A few months earlier as a Senior in high school I was playing offense, defense, and on all special teams. I did not miss a play unless we were way ahead during the fourth quarter. Now, I was looking at a few moments of playing time in my first game. However, I was excited, I had survived camp and now was going to be putting on a college jersey. The trip was going to last about three hours. There was a nice Greyhound bus idling in the parking lot. I watched as the offensive and defensive starters loaded the bus. I already knew that I would not be getting on the bus. Since the number of players making the trip would be more than the capacity of the bus a few other players and myself would be taking an alternative means of travel. That means of travel was a good old fashion station wagon! It was not pea green, like the Griswald's, but the design was the same. To make the trip even more memorable, two other players and myself would be in the very back seat facing backwards! At least I was in a side seat. If you have never traveled a significant distance facing the opposite of the way you are traveling than it's hard to explain the feeling you have every time the brakes are hit harder than usual, or when you start to pass another vehicle of when that 18-wheeler is on your bumper at 70 MPH. We safely made the trip and fortunately for me I was able to ride on the bus for all the remaining road games that season. The trip back was much better as we beat the Gamecocks 11-10 in what was considered a major upset and one that also would propel us to the National Championship.

DO NOT ACT A FOOL: I had drunk a few beers during the summer before my Senior year in high school, but never during any of my sports seasons. I just did not want anything effecting my performance and I was under the assumption that most other players felt like that. I knew that was not completely true but found it to be a lot less true for college players. Looking back, I now understand the maturity level that a person can reach in a hurry after one leaves the structed, and sometimes sheltered, life of grade school. That maturity can let a person make choices that they can handle much better as a college student than as a high school student. With that being said, I found out several players in college drink alcohol, smoke, stayed out late, and was able to bring their "A" game at practice the next day. College coaches know this. They do not go looking in bars or other places to catch players. However, players and coaches both know that if you mess up publicly there will be a price to pay. This story involves two players that did not follow that unwritten rule. When this event happened, the football team was around 6-1 or 7-1 and had been told that if we won the rest of our games we would be going to the playoffs. Excitement was high. Practices were good. Most players were focused. Most. I did not learn what had happened until the next morning, but as soon as I heard I knew something bad was about to happen later. Two players had gotten drunk. They had made it back into the dorm without getting caught but made the unwise decision to go into a dorm room of another player and harass him. This player was an introvert and did everything as straight as an arrow. I do not know the exact details of the harassment, but it upset him enough that he went and told the assistant coach that lived in the dorm. The coach then goes to the room of the two drunk players and finds them passed out. He has a hard time awakening them to get details of what has happened. Needless to say he is not pleased, and none of the coaching staff is pleased after finding out what happened. Practice the next day is brutal. Nothing different than normal as almost every practice was brutal. At the end of every practice, we would gather as a team while the head coach, and sometimes assistants, give their assessment of the day's practice, reminders, news etc. After all of that there is one other piece of business that needs to be taken care of. Coach Andrews begins talking about pride, representing, sacrificing, team goals, opportunities that are before us and then it shifts to not being selfish, making bad decisions, immaturity, and not letting your actions affect the team. He then tells everyone, like no one already knew, that two players have embarrassed the team and that they will have to pay a price because of their actions. At the same time he is talking, the players can see two assistant coaches pulling their whistles out from under their shirts and having a look come across their face that struck terror into those of us who were not in trouble. The two players were offensive lineman which obviously meant they were larger than most and were not in as good of shape as say a receiver or running back. The rest of the team was dismissed and went to the dressing room. The dressing room was up a slight hill about twenty feet higher than the playing field. Well, some of us were very curious as to what was about to happen, so we were hanging out outside the dressing room watching the "attention getter" take place. It started with the players at the goal line sprinting until one of the coaches blew a whistle. At the sound of the whistle the players would have to lounge belly first on to the ground. They would then have to immediately get up and start sprinting again until the next whistle. The players would usually only get about ten yards down the field in between whistles. They made it down the field once and back again. By the time they had made it back they were just about down and out, but the coaches were not. Seeing how the players could hardly get on their feet the coaches begin to help them by grabbing them under their shoulder pads and throwing them forward. As this sequence started another assistant noticed several of us players watching from the dressing room. He started sprinting up the hill saying, "if you are going to watch then you can just join them!" It is amazing how many players could get through a small door in record time as no one was wanting to join them. No one knew what happened after that point. The two players left during the middle of the night.

MISSISSIPPI MUD & CONCRETE: It is March of 1972. Since high school, I have spent one quarter at Livingston University playing football, and one quarter at Northwest Junior College not doing anything except going to school after the baseball program was dropped. A 100 mile a day round trip to Phil Campbell had gotten old. There was only one thing I could do, go to work full time. Fortunately, I had an uncle, Lamar Pitts, who was working for a steel building company in Columbus, Mississippi. The manager of the company had told him to see if he could find a helper since their business was increasing. It would be physical work most of the time but sometimes it would be inside carpentry work and painting.

After about two months of working with Lamar. Two other uncles and my father started working for the steel building company and I was also able to get my best friend on as a helper also. By this time, the summer months had rolled in and we were doing mostly outside work. The work that all of us did was to dig foundations, pour the concrete, and then do the inside work. A completely different crew put up the steel building.

After the corners for the building had been established, Carlos Flynn and I, would start digging the trenches for the footings for the outside area of the building. The footings would be about 8 inches deep and 16 to 20 inches wide. The company did not own a trench digger. Carlos, me, and two shovels were the trench diggers. The location that we were doing most of our work that summer was about thirty miles south of Columbus. The soil in that part of Mississippi was different from what most soil is in the south. Even during the dry summer season, the soil had a mud like texture to it. When you would dig into the soil you could get a shovel full of soil, but when you went to discard it about half of the soil would remain on your shovel. This meant that it would take about twice as long to dig footings in that soil than it would in almost any other type of soil. It was very frustrating.

After the footings were completed the boundaries of the building would be put up with 2" X 8" X 12' planks. These planks had to be exact and would require stubs for braces on the outside about every 6 inches. Again, Carlos and I did most of the physical work for this step but under the watchful eye of one of my uncles. After this step was completed a plastic sheeting, to keep moisture from coming through the concrete had to be put down along with rebar in a grid form for reinforcement. Depending on the size of the building we would also put down sets of planks ten feet from each other in a parallel line with the outside of the building. A lot of hard, physical work, in brutal heat and sun, and this was before the actual pouring of the concrete.

As the concrete is poured into the prepared area some workers are using steel rakes to spread it out. When enough concrete in inside the forms, two workers, guess who, would use a straight 2' X 4' board, called a screed board to level the concrete. The proper technique for this would be to move the board right and left while pulling on the concrete toward you. It would require several pulls just to get a small section of concrete level. Since the concrete would start hardening fast during the summer, once the concrete was coming out of the truck there was no resting or breaks until it was leveled. 80% of the time I worked there the digging of trenches, preparing foundations, and the pouring of concrete was what I did.

At times we also had to bust up old concrete with sledgehammers to prepare a site for a new foundation. However, Carlos and I did learn some carpentry skills, like how to hang ceiling tiles, sawing and placing floorboards, and putting up paneling on walls.

When the middle of August arrived, I had to decision to make. I could stay with this company and begin to learn more carpentry skills, or I could give college another chance. I really liked the inside work of a carpenter. Watching a project come together was very satisfying. However, I still had the need to be an athlete inside me. Because of the lessons I had learned through the hard work of the past several months I knew it was time to get serious and go back to college.

The next two years would be challenging in a lot of ways, but I had matured, I had tasted the real world, and I would draw from those experiences to get me though the upcoming challenges.

JEALOUSY: I was socially awkward as an early teenager. It was during my junior year before I went on my first date. I liked girls but at the time I liked sports more and my priority was to be the best I could be in every sport I attempted. As I got older my football skills increased. As a freshman I started the last four games of that season as the nose guard on defense. My sophomore year I began the season as the starting center on offense and a linebacker on defense. I listened to my coaches, never talked bad about them to my parents or other players and tried to do whatever they asked of me. I do want to make this statement. I often complained as to how tough practices would be sometimes, but nothing toward the character of the men.

After my freshman year, the Sulligent football program had just completed a four-year record of 34 wins, 4 losses and 1 tie. Two of the loses and the tie was to Fayette High School, a much bigger school than Sulligent. There had been a lot of talent in the football program those four years, but there had also been unprecedented leadership with each senior class. Going into my sophomore year, most of the talent was gone, but also, most of the leadership was gone.

Two of our most talented players, who were seniors quit early in the year. Too many of the remaining seniors were more interested in their girlfriends and partying than football, as they would often make plans and talk about their girlfriends during practice. We won two games and lost eight games that season.

A football booster club had formed before the season started mainly to help finance the football team with pregame meals and a banquet at the end of the season.

I went to the banquet – alone. There was a guest speaker, and a nice meal. The booster club had planned to give out two trophies. One trophy for the best offensive player and one trophy for the best defensive player. The awards had been voted on by the club members. The first trophy for best offensive player went to Kenneth Humbers. This was a no brainer. Kenneth was also a sophomore who was a bruising fullback and who was really our only offensive spark that year. As I sat in my seat waiting for the announcement of the best defensive player, I began to think of two people from whom would be chosen for the award. The club president announced the winner, "Jerry Pitts". I sat there in a surreal moment, not believing that I had just heard my name called.

There was also a moment of silence before I rose from my seat and went forward to receive the trophy.

With the awarding of the trophies the banquet came to an end. The head coach, Kenneth, and I were having as picture made. The head coach made the comment, "I am not sure what to think about sophomores winning these awards." That comment would stick with me and motivate me throughout high school.

The award did two things for me. I accepted the award and the pressure from winning it to improve. I had a good season but was not sure that I was the best defensive player, but I was determined to be the best defensive player my next two seasons. The other thing it did for me was to make me a target for the upperclassmen, both juniors and seniors, as they immediately became jealous of my getting the award. I did not hang out with any of them. In their minds since I stayed home most of the time or just hung to with other sophomores like myself, I was inferior to them and the last thing I deserved was a trophy. There were a lot of snide remarks made to me like, "I am surprised you are not home polishing your trophy" and such. I ignored most of the comments. Anything I could have said would not have been accepted by them as a reason I should have won the trophy. I stayed humble and quiet about it but worked harder than ever to get better. By the start of my junior season there was not any doubt who the best defensive player on the team was and I owe a lot of that to the jealousy that was displayed toward me.

WATER: Gatorade, Powerade, energy drinks, supplements for before a workout, supplements for after a workout, ice baths, etc. In today's athletic world there is no limit to the items that are pushed on an athlete in the name of helping a person to be better, stronger, faster, to recover quicker, and to avoid injury. Yes, water is still among those items but even water had a late introduction into the athletic arena.

The first water that was available at a football practice at Sulligent was during my sophomore year, 1968. Up until that time there was not any type of hydration during practice. Did we need water? Yes, we did. We craved water. The town of Sulligent had two Artesian wells. This is a well in which water from the ground is constantly flowing out of a pipe, without a pump, if not capped. After almost every practice I would go to these wells and drink so much water I would almost throw up.

Before the start of one practice on a hot day in August, the head coach assembled all the players and said he had an announcement. We would start having a water break. We all became excited, but there were ground rules. Every player would only get one ration of water. If we acted "like dummies" the water breaks would be cut out. Practice started. After about an hour we were going to receive our first water break. The coaches brought out a five-gallon steel bucket filled with water. Inside the bucket was a ladle. Each player would use the same ladle, get one scoop of water, drink it, and hand the ladle to the next player.

Not a single player every turned down the water.

HOOPS: After the 1966 football season the aura over Sulligent was one of great satisfaction, comfort, and blessing. The Blue Devils had just completed the single greatest football season in the history of the school. Sulligent had had undefeated football seasons in the past but never a 10-0 season plus being named 2A State Champions by The Birmingham News. At that time there were only 4 classifications of schools which meant there were about 120 schools in each classification. Things were peaceful as basketball season approached. A lot of the talent that was on the football team were also talented basketball players, but most of that basketball season would be spent talking about the previous football season.

I had a novel interest in basketball. I had never played the sport or had every had any imaginary games or drills outside. I would occasionally watch some NBA games on television, but those broadcasts were few and far between. My father never talked about basketball, neither did any of my close friends. I did not have anything against basketball, it was just that my heart was in football, with baseball being a close second.

About a week after football season was over, I was riding the bus home every day, going to my room, doing little studying and mostly wasting time. One day my father needed to go to town after he got home from work. He told me to go with him. I was ready. I liked being around him and was always up for a trip to town.

I do not remember the purpose of the trip, but I can visually see in my mind the event that unfolded on the way back home. Shortly into the trip, without any previous conversation, my father says, "I want you to go out for basketball tomorrow". After a slight pause, I responded with, "I don't think I want to play basketball tomorrow". After an even slighter pause my father says, "you must not have heard me. I want you to go out for basketball tomorrow". End of conversation. Message delivered and taken.

At the time I was puzzled about my father's sudden interest in basketball and in particularly why he was insisting that I go out for the sport. Later, after a few seasons of basketball, it was obvious that it was one of the greatest decisions every made on my behalf. My father did not have a high school diploma, but he was blessed with much wisdom. He knew what my goals were as they related to football. He also wanted me to experience a better life than him. He knew that I would not develop as a football player if I did not keep active in some form during the entire calendar year. I was active during the summer. I was active during football and baseball seasons. There was nothing to do during the winter except play basketball.

Through basketball drills and games, I developed and improved my hand and eye coordination, my quickness, my feet reaction, my leaping ability, my endurance, my muscles, and my competitive spirit. I soon learned to love the game. My love for it did not surpass football or baseball, but I wanted to do my best and I wanted to win. By the beginning of spring training football practice, I was already a better football player.

Thanks Dad.

NEWSWORTHY: Life has some unique turns often when you least expect it. I loved little league baseball and while most other young boys that I was around did not want any part of playing the catcher's position, I fell in love with it. It was exciting putting the equipment on. It was like I was going into battle. I knew that for a baseball team to be successful the team must have dominant pitching, back by solid defense. However, the defensive position that was involved in every pitch, of every game, was the catcher's position. No game was every boring when I was catching. I played a few games in the outfield and some games it was so hard to stay focused, but if I did not stay focused while catching, bad things could happen.

One summer, when I guess I was about 12 years old, we had just finished little league practice for the day and the coach had brought us inside the dressing room. I am sure he had some announcements, but I do not remember what they were. Before we were finished a man named Joe Acee entered the dressing room. Mr. Acee, or I should say Coach Acee, was a legend in Sulligent, Lamar county, and most of Alabama. He was the winningest football coach in Sulligent high school football history.

He was also a World War II veteran, and an accomplished author. Coach Acee was currently writing newspaper articles for the county newspaper that was published weekly. Upon entering the dressing room, he asked Jimmy Graham, who was the current baseball coach at Sulligent, a few questions about the upcoming little league season. Coach Acee then asked Coach Graham to pick out someone for a picture. Coach Graham looked around and then asked Coach Acee, "which one"? Coach Acee replied, "preferably, one with a baseball cap on".

I wore my baseball coach constantly during the summer months, not just during baseball practice. I was sitting quietly back in a corner, but I had heard the conversation between the two men, and I realized that I was the only boy in the dressing room with a baseball cap on. Mr. Acee pointed at me and said, "how about that one"? It was fine with Coach Graham and he seemed relieved that he had not had to make the decision as to which boy to pick. I stood up, Coach Graham gave me a bat, I got into a batter's stance, Coach Graham put his hands on the bat like he was instructing me, and Mr. Acee took the picture.

The article and the picture appeared in the next edition of the newspaper. However, unlike the trophy I received as the Most Valuable Defensive player after my sophomore season, there was not the slightest hint of jealousy toward me. I was humble about the incident, and no one ever said anything about it.

TIGHT FIT: Sometime during the early 1950's Sulligent, and some of the other local communities built new gymnasiums for their schools. The gyms looked like three large quonset huts pushed together. These buildings were made from metal, not insulated, without air conditioning, and was heated by a large coal burning heater in one corner. They were used for physical education classes and for basketball. There was plenty of room at end of the courts and adequate room on the sidelines between players and fans. However, the were generally cold and not healthy because of the manner of heat used.

These buildings lasted around a dozen years before they began to fall into disrepair. Most in the area were condemned for use. This created a dilemma for the basketball programs in the area. Without an adequate gymnasium and not any money in the budget to build a new gym the administrations turned to their only other option, the high school auditorium. The administrations knew that between local funding and state funding it would take about three years to save enough money to build new gymnasiums. In the meantime, they did not just want to suspend the playing of basketball. In Lamar County integration had not taken place at this time. There were five schools in the county. Four all White and one all Black. Sulligent and Vernon would move away from playing in the Quonset huts to the auditoriums. Sets of bleachers were put down each side of the auditorium. To save as much space as possible the bleachers consisted of only three rows. The out of bounds stripes were painted six inches from the end of the bleachers. This meant that when a game was being played spectators on the bottom row would have the feet and legs on the playing surface. The backboards were located about three feet from the end walls. One wall was solid, the other wall had a stage on it. This meant that the out of bounds line on the ends of the court would be about one foot from the wall. The result would be that when a player was inbounding the basketball after a made basket or a turnover that they would be in the court of play instead of completely out of bounds. Officials had no choice but to overlook the sideline and end line rules violations.

Another factor that came into play during a game was the height of the ceiling. Long passes from one end of the court to the other end were next to impossible because the ball would often hit the ceiling and that would be called a turnover. Finally, the playing floor was made of wood, but since it had been waxed and oiled for years, the traction was not what that of a normal wooden basketball court would be.

Yes, there were a lot of players going into the bleachers chasing errant passes, players slamming into the walls and even ending up on stage when driving hard to the basket or trying to play tight defense. However, the seasons went on and those of us who played basketball were just thankful to have a place to play.

IN 1966 Sulligent and Vernon each got identical new gymnasiums. They were modest by what one might expect of today's standards but after playing in quonest huts and auditoriums they seemed like the Taj Mahal and we loved them.

PIING PONG AND BARBELLS: Like I stated before my father was full of wisdom. He never bragged on me directly very much, but I knew he was proud of me. I looked up to him and rarely questioned his actions when I was a child and early teenager. The same year that he had "wanted" me to go out for basketball he also knew that even through playing basketball would help me develop my body in a lot of ways, it would not add much muscle mass and weight to my body. Hoping to increase my muscle mass, body weight, and strength he came home from work one day with a used barbell set. It was a Sears and Roebuck model. It was concrete wrapped in plastic. The set consisted of one long bar and two hand bars. The weights were in increments of 5, 10 and 25 pounds. The total weight of the set was 125 pounds.

I began using the set at least five days a week. Military press, squats, calf rises, bicep curls, upright rows, and occasionally bench press which required me to lay on the floor since I did not have a proper weight bench. I experienced a growth spurt and increased strength in a few months. However, I soon got to the point that I did not have enough total weight to challenge me so I would have to do about 5 times the normal reps for a set to see any benefit.

The weight set was not fancy, but it was exactly what I needed at the exact time in life that I needed it. Schools did not have weight training programs during this time, so this gave me an advantage over most of the other boys. Two years later my father would show his wisdom again.

On my fifteenth birthday my father bought me a ping pong table. Everyone loves ping pong. I was excited and I knew my friends would be also. However, my father did not buy the ping pong table just for my recreational enjoyment, he also knew it would make me a better athlete. Ping pong requires much concentration, eye and hand coordination, and quickness. It requires forehand and backhand ability and the ability of changing from a hard slam to a gentle touch. At the time all I was thinking about was being able to beat my friends. Playing ping pong only increased my already competitive nature. The reality was playing ping pong benefitted me as a hitter in baseball, the ability to dribble a basketball without looking at the ball, the ability to follow a running back down the line of scrimmage while fending off blockers without having to look at the blockers. Who knew I could develop as an athlete and have fun doing it? My father did.

Thanks Dad

BELL RINGER: I never had a nickname. None of my close friends did either. In today's world it seems like almost all athletes have an aka. Being an introvert, I was not wanting attention to myself by having a nickname. However, it did seem that every person that I knew that did have a nickname that the nickname given to them fitted them perfectly. Growing up almost all the boys referred to each other by their last name. I honestly cannot remember any of my male friends every calling me Jerry.

After the 1974 season in which had had a great season, I was named All GSC Conference and most outstanding defensive player for the Tigers I felt like I had almost reached my potential as a college football player. I had the opportunity to become better, but it was postponed because I had to have major surgery on my right shoulder that caused me to miss the off-season workouts and spring training.

As fall practice began for the 1975 season there was high expectations for our team and myself as I always had a goal of doing better than I had the season before. During fall camp an article appeared in the paper about me in which my head coach was talking about me as a player. He referred to me as a "bell-ringer". This term is not used very often today in the football vocabulary, but it was the term used to describe a defensive player who was a hard hitter, who punished his opponents, and was consistent at doing it.

Contact had always been my favorite part of football. Growing up idolizing players like Dick Butkus, Ray Nitschke, and Deacon Jones, it was natural that I wanted to be feared as a hitter. I never backed away from contact. That does not mean that I won every battle, but it was not because I was afraid of the physicality of the battle.

One of my friends, Mickey Lindsey, who was a defensive back, and who was great at poking fun at his friends immediately started giving me a hard time about the "bell-ringer" comment that had been made in the paper. He said it so much that some of the other players started calling me that also. I had my one and only nickname. Although, I downplayed it and never referred to myself with that term I was proud of it. That was who I was, and it seemed if I had achieved a goal by someone like my head coach referring to me as a "bell-ringer".

ROAD TRIPS: In my many years as a player, teacher, coach, and administrator I seen many men try to be fathers. However, many did not try at all. Too many of those men tried to be a father by giving their children money, material possessions, fees for camps and trips, the latest phone or other technological device, but they failed as fathers. They never gave them what really mattered, significant one on one time. There is not anything wrong with providing your children with things they need and want but it should not be a substitute for time. It is easy to see a child that is blessed with a father who gives them time and attention and those who do not receive it.

My mother and father sacrificed a lot for my sister and me so that we could have the things we needed. We did not have a lot of extras, but we did know that we had their love and attention.

My father wanted to expose me to things outside of Sulligent. He did this as much as the money would allow him to. The first road trip was a spontaneous one. My uncle and cousin showed up at our house just before noon on a Saturday in October. He talked to my father and convinced him to go with them to Birmingham to see Auburn and Georgia Tech play football. Of course, my father was taking me along. We headed out for Birmingham and Legion Field. At that time, it took over three hours to make that trip. Today you can make it in a little over two hours. The little detail that I was not aware of was that kickoff for that game was about 30 minutes after we left. The trip took us through several towns, all with plenty of traffic lights and low speed limits. Winding roads, often with very few passing zones. We finally pulled into the parking lot of Legion Field. A lot of the fans were leaving the massive stadium. I was in awe that young men got to play football in such a facility. We walked right through the gates without any tickets. Why were we able to do that? They were two minutes left in the game and the gatekeepers had opened the gates to make it easier for fans to exit. We went in and sat on one of the lower rows of bleachers. The players were muddy as it had rained a good bit in the days leading up to the game. Georgia Tech was winning 17-3 and that would be the final score. About five minutes after we sat down the game was over. We headed back to the car. Before we headed back, we stopped at a KFC for chicken. It was the first time that I had KFC chicken. I do not know if it was because the chicken was so good or if I was just starving, but it seems like I can still taste how delicious that chicken was. Looking back, I believe the main purpose of the trip was for my father and his brother to have some quality time as they did a lot of talking and shared a pint of whiskey during the trip. It was a long day, but it did make me hunger for more experiences like that.

A couple of years later my daddy would begin taking me to football games at Starkville, Mississippi, Oxford, Mississippi, and Tuscaloosa, Alabama. Tickets were easy to come by and I have the ticket stubs to almost every game we went to. He would always buy us a program and sometimes but me a souvenir. Of course, the hot dogs were always better at a ball game than anywhere else. Unlike the Birmingham trip, we would get to the stadium as early as possible to watch warm-ups. I would go down toward the bottom of the stadium to get as close to the action of the warm-ups as I could. We never left early, savoring every moment, even if the team we were rooting for was losing. Time. He gave me his time. After a long 40-hour work week that included a daily 90-minute round trip to work and back home, whenever possible he gave up his Saturdays to give me time. These trips reinforced my dreams to play college football. I would envision the days that I would be playing in front of fans that would come from miles around to cheer us on. It gave me a work ethic that would give me the opportunity to make those dreams come true.

One of the benefits to being a high school football coach was that colleges would give you two free tickets to their home games. Each university would allot a certain number of tickets to give away. This would come out of their recruiting fund. The only requirement was to call the university, request the tickets, tell them what school you were coaching at, and tell them exactly what position(s) you coached. However, you had to call quickly once the university started accepting calls, as these tickets would be distributed quickly.

I used these tickets to help repay my father for the time that he gave me. I was giving him time back by taking him to games. Sometimes I would use them for my son and sometimes another coach and myself would use them. You would not know from one season to the next were you would be sitting. Some years the seats would be I the end zone, some years in the upper deck on the 50-yard line, sometimes on row 3 in the bottom of the stadium on the 10 yard line. Wherever they were, they were free, and we could enjoy college football.

ATLANTA STADIUM: In my early teens during the summer, I hungered for baseball. It was hard to find. We would play only 10 to 12 summer league games. Televised baseball games of major league baseball were only on Saturdays and baseball on the radio came across on the AM stations. Some nights I would be able to pick up the broadcast of the Cincinnati Reds and some nights I would be able to pick up the broadcast of the St. Louis Cardinals and some nights I would not be able to pick up either broadcast. Often the broadcasts would fade out for several pitches before coming back on. However, listening to these games on radio was beneficial for me. Since it was a radio broadcast the announcers had to constantly be talking. They had to be good enough for the listener to be able to envision what was going on as if the listener were in the stands watching. They would talk strategy to the point it was like taking a lesson in baseball 101. They would describe in such detail how the players would pitch, hit, field, and throw that you could almost feel their sweat. Yes, they were that good.

I had little interest in the Milwaukee Braves. I had never seen them on television and can not remember listening to a game on the radio that they were involved in. All of that changed in the spring of 1966. The Braves were moving to Atlanta.

Major League baseball was coming to the South. Major league baseball pre-season training had taken place in Florida for many years, but as the season started all the teams went to the North, Midwest, and West. This time a team would only be going a little bit north to the State of Georgia and fans across the southeast became instant fans of the Braves.

The Braves were a good team in 1966 and they had two future Hall of Fame players on the team in Eddie Matthews and Hank Aaron. The city of Atlanta had built a stadium in less than a year for only $18 million that seated 50,000 fans. Major league baseball had not had a new stadium built in several years, but the Atlanta stadium would become a prototype for several other cities to follow. The stadium was one mile from downtown Atlanta and completely changed the skyline of the city. That same year the NFL granted Atlanta an expansion team, the Falcons, and they would also play in the stadium. These two events would bolt Atlanta to become a metropolitan city and greatly increase their population.

Growing up I could only imagine seeing a Major League baseball game in person and even through the Braves were now in Atlanta they still seemed a lifetime away. That all changed when just before the season started my father came to me and said, "we need to pick out a weekend that we can go see the Braves". I believe I stopped breathing for a few seconds. I was so excited I could hardly react but eventually responded with an "yes sir"! The only challenge was to find a home series on the weekend my father got paid. He was paid every other week, so I had to search through the Braves schedule for a series that matched his payday. I found one and I could not have found one any better.

We would leave on a Friday, find a hotel close to Atlanta, go to the game on Saturday and return home on Saturday. What made the series I found so special was that the opponent was the Los Angeles Dodgers. The Dodgers were a powerhouse during the 60's and were filled with many stars like Sandy Koufax, Don Drysdale, and Maury Wills, to name a few. What made it even better was that the Braves and Dodgers would be playing a doubleheader that Saturday. Not just a normal doubleheader but a day/night doubleheader. The first game would start at noon and the second game would start at 8 p.m.

After my father got home from work we immediately headed for Atlanta. A long 6-hour journey was ahead for us. The entire family went, but only my father and me would be going to the game, while my mother and sister would be staying at the hotel and be entertained most of the day by a swimming pool. The drive was challenging as we went through so many small towns on the way, and it was approaching 11 p.m. as we headed into downtown Atlanta. Suddenly, we cleared the city and there it was in all its glory, ATLANTA STADIUM! It looked like a giant spaceship. It was a complete circle with slanted white columns and a partial blue roof. Enormous light was given off by the stadium lights and the lights surrounding the outside of the stadium. I was 13 but I was jumping up and down on the back seat with excitement. I really could not believe what was in front of my eyes. I wanted to pull in and go to the game that was being played. My father told me that the game was nearly over and that we needed to find a motel.

We learned a lesson that night. When a visiting major league baseball team is in town, especially on the weekends, motel rooms are hard to find. Two hours later, after driving through all parts of Atlanta, we found a hotel, with a vacancy, 20 miles outside of Atlanta. We would learn another lesson later about big-time baseball in a city.

My father and I left the motel around 10 a.m. headed toward Atlanta stadium. After we got there, we discovered that there were about 8 locations outside of the stadium, "ticket-booths", that one could purchase game tickets. My father and I looked over the options for the tickets he could afford. With tickets in hand, we headed for the inside of the stadium.

As we walked through the turnstile, I could barely see the other side of the stadium through an entrance. The closer I got the more I could see until finally I was completely inside the stadium and gazed over the beauty that was before my eyes. Thousands of blue seats, two giant scoreboards, long dugouts, and the beauty of a finely manicured grass infield. After we found our seats, I made my way down to where other fans were gathered close to the field attempting to get autographs from players and coaches. I did not get any autographs that day but would get several over the coming years as we would make this a yearly event. It was a beautiful day with clear skies and moderate temperatures. The Braves won the game and Hank Aaron had hit a home run. Since the game was over before 3 p.m. my father decided we would go back to the hotel for a few hours before coming back for the second game.

Since we had arrived at the stadium about two hours before the start of the first game and had had plenty of time to get tickets and enjoy the happenings before the first pitch my father decided we would leave at a time that would have us arriving about an hour before game time of the second game. Remember, this was our first time dealing with professional sports.

After parking we walked to the first available ticket booth. No one was in it. Weird. We walked to the next, and the next, and the next. They were all empty. Finally, we found a ticket booth with a person in it. We told him we needed tickets. His response was, "SOLD OUT". My heart fell to my feet, my mouth wide open, and tears began to form. We started walking around the stadium looking for anyone who might have extra tickets to sell. Nothing. Game time was rapidly approaching. Eventually, no one was outside the stadium but a few lost souls with disappointment hanging on their sleeves.

My daddy had a lot of wisdom. He had joined the Navy at age 17 and had served most of his time in the Pacific arena and on the coast of California. Considering the devastating situation, he was very calm. The game had started and no one was entering the stadium. He seemed he was looking for something specific, but I was not asking any questions. We approached a gate. There was a single man there at the turnstile. I was close enough to hear my daddy say to the man, "my son really wants to see this game", while at the same time he was pulling some bills out of his pocket. I do not know the amount that he had in his hand, but the guy took it and then looked to his right and looked to his left. No one was in sight. He said, "y'all, step this way" and directed us behind the turnstile and into the stadium. We walked to the upper deck hoping to be less conspicuous and found an entrance into the stadium. Over 50,000 people were in attendance.

We learned several things that night. One could buy tickets in advance, and you better consider who the visiting team is and who is the starting pictures are for both teams. The starting pitcher for the Dodgers that night was Don Drysdale. He was in his prime on the way to a Hall of Fame career. This was the first time the Dodgers had visited Atlanta and although there were only 30,000 fans for the noon game the other three games of the series were all sold out.

We stood up the entire game, sometimes leaning on the entrance wall. It was a classic game with the Braves winning 2-1. Both starting pictures were dominant, but the highlight of the game was catcher, and future Hall of Famer, Joe Torre of the Braves throwing out speedster, and record holder for stolen bases in a season, Maury Wills, twice while trying to steal second base.

We headed back to the motel. We were tired, but it was a good tired. It had been a great day. The Braves had won, but more importantly my father and I had bonded even closer. I have been to see the Braves several times since 1966, with my father, son, daughter, friends, and my wife Leslie. This day would be among the tops of the trips but rivaled with another. In 2002 my father had been diagnosed with prostrate cancer. He had it under control, but also had some other health problems. One Sunday evening I was visiting him and talk, as usual, evolved to sports. Suddenly I had the idea that we should drive to Atlanta the next day to see the Braves play, spend the night after the game and come home on Tuesday. We started talking more about details and finally decided we would enjoy the game more if we left immediately, spend Sunday night in Atlanta and be well rested for the game. So that is what we did. Since we were already in Atlanta, we were able to tour the stadium that morning. The tour took us to all parts of the stadium, the press box, locker rooms, bull pens, and even to the playing field and the dugouts. I have some great pictures from that tour and from the game later. The Braves won and my father really enjoyed himself. It made me feel good to be able to treat him to an experience that he had given me 36 years earlier.

He died six months later from pneumonia.

FATHER KNOWS BEST: One of the best ways for a parent to show a child that they love them is to say "no". It is automatic for a parent to say no if the child is young and is about to do something that would put them in danger. However, it is hard for some parents to say no to a child in their early years even if they know that by saying no the child will benefit from that answer or instruction. Too many parents will say yes too often and about too many things in hope that this will increase the child's love for them. It usually has the opposite effect. A child that hears yes all, or most, of the time grows up without boundaries and usually with a lack of respect for his or her parents or authority figures. Telling a child no, shows wisdom and discernment even if the child becomes upset with the parent. A wise parent needs to know when to say yes and when to say no and that that no always means no, not just sometimes and then the answer changes to yes.

I cannot remember being told no very often growing up. I believe that it was because I was told no a lot as a youngster and by the time of my life that I can remember things I did not do things that I knew I would be told no or ask for things that I knew we could not afford, so I did not have to be told no. My daddy rarely negotiated and when my mother said no, I knew neither would change their mind.

However, there was one time I was told no, and it saved my life.

August 1971. I was headed to Livingston University to attend college and play football. I had only been to Livingston University once in my life. My head high school coach had played football there and he had taken me on a visit to meet the coaches and see the campus. I was not impressed. I was disillusioned as to why I had not been offered a scholarship to an SEC school. I was named by the Birmingham News as on of the best 11 players in the state. There are several reasons that I know now why that did not happen. I also know that it was God's plan, and His plans are always better than ours, for me to go to Livingston University and be a Tiger. They offered me a scholarship and I signed it.

My daddy drove me to the campus on a Saturday morning to check in, unpack, and get settled in. It was only a two hour trip but it seemed much longer. There was little between Sulligent and Livingston other than trees. The town was about the same size as Sulligent. It did not fill my expectations of what a college town would be like. After everything was in my dorm room, there was a team meeting scheduled so my daddy told me good luck, shook my hand, and with as much pride as a parent could have, looked me in the eye and said, "I love you".

If the town or campus or football facilities did not seem like what I imagined college would be, it would not be long for me to find out that it certainly was not high school anymore. The intensity level was much higher, the talent level was higher, the practices were tougher, the meetings lasted forever, and the cussing was coming from every direction. We had physicals and received equipment the same day we moved in. At the end of the day, we had our first practice in shorts and helmets. It was intense. We practiced twice the next two days in shorts and helmets before putting on full pads. Things then got real serious.

There were not any other students on campus and would not be for six weeks. There was one place to get a hamburger in town, but no one had any time to visit it. It was a lonely and desolate place and the day consisted of breakfast at 7:30, meeting at 8:00, practice at 9:30, lunch at 12:30, meeting at 2:00, practice at 3:30, supper at 6:30, meeting at 7:00 until 9:00, lights out at 10:00. Every day was like this. 100% football. There were not any cell phones, long distance calls cost money, so you were limited to have conversations with people you had been around all day.

I was physically able to hang with the other players, but all the players were physical, and the speed level of the practices was much higher than high school. I guess we had had a pretty good week of practice because on Friday of that first week the coaches told us that we would not have practice on Sunday. We would have a meeting after supper, but we would have free time until then and that we could invite our parents to visit us if we wanted to. Of course, I invited them along with my girlfriend.

They arrived around 10 on that Sunday morning and we had a good visit for a while. I eventually asked my parents if I could take my girlfriend for a drive. Sure, was their answer. As we drove off, I did not have any destination in mind. I just needed to talk to her. Shortly into the drive I started to cry. Literally crying tears. I began by telling how much I hated being there, how much I hated practice. How much I hated the coaches. We just kept driving and I kept talking. My immaturity was on full display. There is no excuse for my actions, but I did not care. I told her that when we got back, I was going to tell my parents that I was loading up and going home with them.

We had been gone for over an hour by the time we got back to my parents. As soon as we got out of the car my parents knew something was wrong. It did not take me long to get straight to the point. I was leaving and nothing was going to make me stay. I tried to explain how I felt and why I was wanting to leave. My girlfriend and my mother were immediately on my side and were ready to help me pack. My daddy listened, but he wanted a more detailed explanation of the situation. This went on for about an hour before my daddy left. I did not know where he went, but he shortly returned with one of the coaches. I was not expecting that. The coach started talking to me and I was intimidated by him and was vague in my answers to him. After about 45 minutes he got up, agitated, and told me and my dad that "he has got to make a decision" and left.

By this time, my mom and girlfriend were mad at my daddy for not agreeing to take me home. He had not yet said no, but he was searching for everything he could to convince me to stay.

I had a cousin who was four years older than me. He was a great football player. A running back with speed and size. He signed a scholarship with Ole Miss. He made the mistake of moving to Oxford in the summer before practice started in August. He left the team and came home a few days before practice started. He had been severely hazed, as were all freshmen during that time, and decided that college football was not for him. He had a car, so his dad did not have the opportunity to convince him to stay. He was home and was not going back. I may have done the same thing if I had had a car. Of course, I had wrecked mine a few weeks earlier. My cousin went on to have a career in the Air Force. He had the talent to be a star in the SEC, but he did not give himself the chance. Since practice started as soon as we got to campus there was not any free time for hazing to take place. That would come later. My dad reminded me of my cousin. I knew I did not have any real skills except to go to work in a factory, but I was willing to do that if it got me out of Livingston.

Finally, my dad looked at me and said, "trust me", I am not taking you home and you are going to be all right. I did not want to hear that. My mother and girl friend did not want to hear that. But I accepted it. He knew that I had to stay. He knew it would be the best thing for me. And I know it was not easy on him to say that. He could have taken the easy way out and said load up, but he stood strong and saved me from myself.

I finished that season and semester, but I did not return in January. A year later I did return. The experience I has during that year made me understand where I needed to be and what I needed to do, but if my father had not made me stay that first season I never would have gone back.

Thank you, dad.

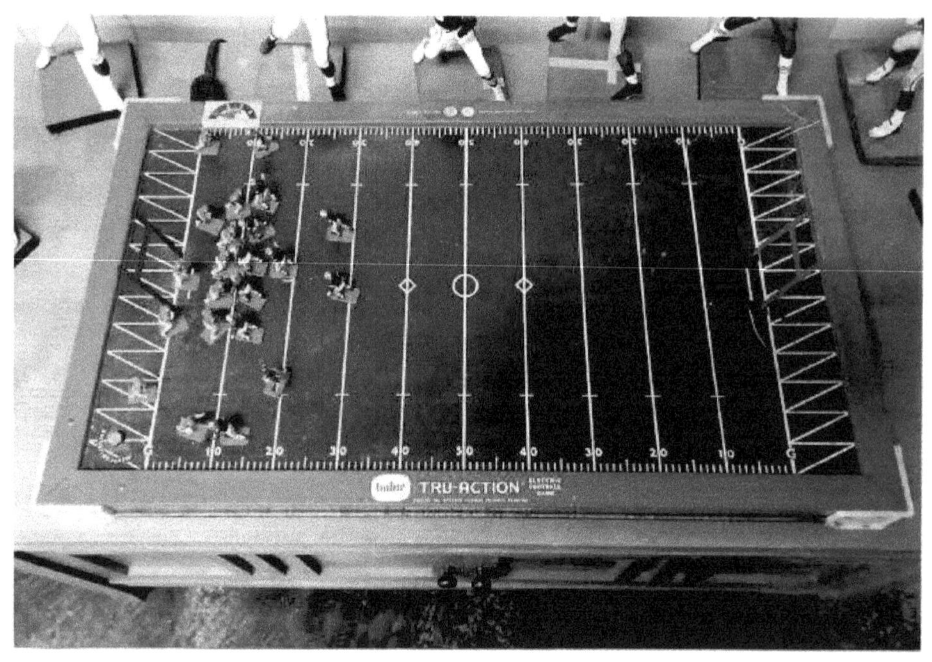

A childhood memory

Given to me by my wife,

Leslie, who has just retrieved

a baseball during batting

practice

My first game as a college

Football player on a team

That would win the

National Championship

An unidentified player enjoys Water, as we all did, no matter The method of drinking it.

Newsworthy

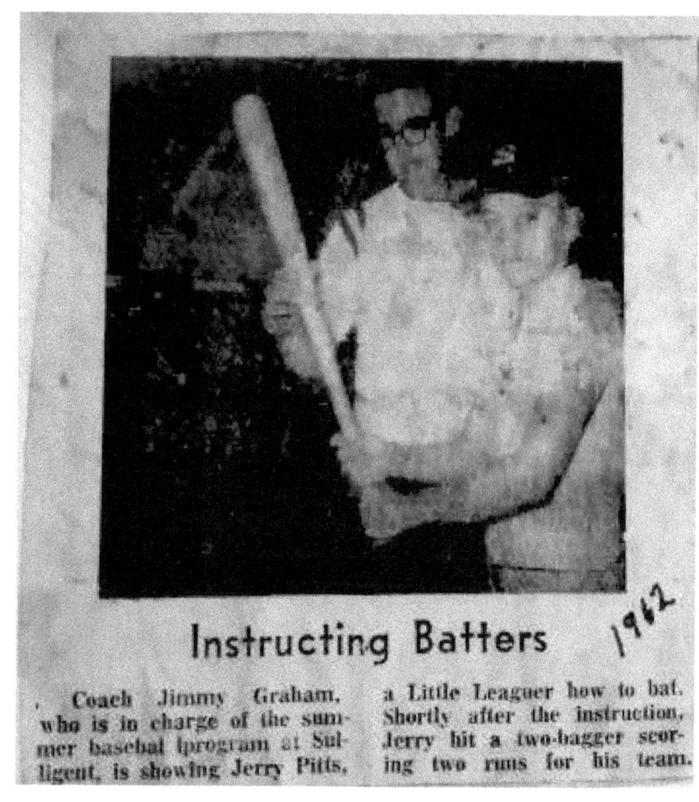

Instructing Batters 1962

Coach Jimmy Graham, who is in charge of the summer basebal lprogram at Sulligent, is showing Jerry Pitts, a Little Leaguer how to bat. Shortly after the instruction, Jerry hit a two-bagger scoring two runs for his team.

The 1971 National Champions – ON the field as a freshman #68

Jerry Pitts 'rings bells' for LU Tigers

Tight ends in the Gulf South Conference had better be wary this fall. They will be facing LU Strong Defensive End Jerry Pitts of Sulligent, who has a reputation as a "Bell-Ringer."

Pitts, an All-GSC and All-District performer a Strong Linebacker last Fall, is lining up in the same position as 1974 but is listed as an end in the Tiger's new 5-2 defensive alignment.

At 6 feet, 215 pounds, Pitts was the leading tackler on the squad in 1974 with 63 solo stops and 45 assists.

"Jerry is a hard worker and hustler, and is a real mature, settled down young man," said LU Head Coach Jim King.

"He is one of the few defensive ends who not only can rush the passer but cover passes also," King added.

Pitts, who is a definite All-American candidate, is one of the few 6 foot players the pros are looking at.

He was Lu's defensive captain against Southern State and will serve as a co-captain against North Alabama along with the seven other Tiger Seniors.

Jerry Pitts

The article that gave me my nickname.

An early road trip with my Father allowed me to watch Bear Bryant (circle) and he Crimson Tide defeat Clemson in Tuscaloosa in 1968

Later, I would continue the road trip tradition with my son, Nathan,and return the favor to my Dad.

1966 Atlanta Stadium. I still vividly remember my first Major League Baseball experience.

Chapter 4

Among Other Things

Randy Johnson, #40, was the first great Black athlete at Sulligent High School

Pre-Game Meals

After Sulligent won the AA State Championship in football in 1966 the head coach moved to another school. That, of course, resulted in a new head coach for the Blue Devils. Like any other coach, he brought his own method of doing things. Some of his coaching, administration, and personality were like the previous coach, but a lot of it was also different.

One major change was that he had all the players stay at school on game day. No one could leave. We all reported to the gym as soon as school was dismissed. Under the previous coach, players had a set time to be back. You left the campus, went either home or to a café to get something to eat, and returned usually about an hour before you left on the bus to go to an away game or if it was a home game, about an hour before you had to go out on the field for pre-game warmups. Most of the time there was not any issue with any of the players getting into any trouble when away from school…..most of the time. However, the new coach wanted a more certain way to contain that. He wanted more focus on the game. He wanted to eliminate distractions in whatever form that might be there for the players. To make this happen he was able to secure funding for pre-game meals. All of this was new to the players, and it took some adjustment. Most did not know how to "focus" on the game that long away from kickoff. The new coach wanted a disciplined approach, which meant very little talking and no horseplay. For the most part players stayed in line. Well, at least while the coaches were in our presence.

About 30 minutes after school had been dismissed all the players had put away any personal possessions and assembled on the bleachers. The coaches would come out, give a few instructions, talk about the opponent, and remind everyone of what was considered proper conduct at the meal.

We had to walk about 300 feet from the gym to the cafeteria and it was kind of like a flock of geese flying south for the winter. The older players and starters were at the point and the younger players and those not expected to play would be further back and out. Being a freshman, I was far back. As each year passed, I moved closer and closer to the front and during my senior year I was often first to eat. Pecking orders exist in many areas of society.

The menu never changed for those four years. A huge, deep fried chicken breast, green beans, mashed potatoes, two rolls, and sweet tea was served. It was good, very good. We were given about 25 minutes to eat and then went back to the gym. Light conversation and even smiling was allowed. I enjoyed these pre-game meals and I think it was beneficial for us.

In 1971 I experienced my first college football pre-game meal. To say it was different from high school pre-game meals is a major underestimate. Since college games are played on Saturdays at different times for kickoffs, a pre-game meal may be served at 8:00 a.m., 10:00 a.m., or 3:00 p.m. They were served 4 hours before kickoff. If the game was a home game, all the players would assemble I the cafeteria at least 15 minutes before mealtime. If the game was away, the players would stay in their motel room and all head toward the restaurant at the same time, again about 15 minutes before serving time.

The similarity between the high school pre-game meal and the college pre-game meal was that each was preceded with a blessing. All similarities, other than the consumption of food, ended there. You walked through the serving line completely quiet. There was about distance of about a person between each player. No one was touching anyone else. No one was even slightly bumping into anyone else. From the moment you entered the serving area until after you had completely left the restaurant you did not open your mouth except to put food in it. You were allowed to respond to a coach if he had spoken to you first.

You did not smile. You barely looked left or right, and you certainly did not look around the room in a curiosity manner. Once you got to your seat you did not start to eat until all the coaches were seated at the front so that they could observe the players. They were not happy. At least that was the appearance that was perceived. Players were on edge not to draw any attention such as dropping a fork or accidentally knocking over a glass.

The meal was steak, baked potato, green beans, and tea. Sounds good? Well, there were not any condiments for the steak. There was not any butter for the potato and the tea was unsweetened. We did have salt, no pepper. However, we were allowed, and encouraged to put honey on our steak. While the players struggled to get the food down in the condition it was served, we also had to watch as the coaches had ample steak sauce to pick from, mounds of butter, and of course, sugar for their tea.

I'm not sure why the coaches, both high school and college, picked menus that they did for their pre-game meals. I often wished that I had asked. I assume the high school meal was based somewhat on economics since we were an economically disadvantaged school and I assume since our college head coach had played for Bear Bryant it is probably what they had for pre-game meals at Alabama. A lot of pressure was lifted after completing the college pre-game meal. Almost all focus had been on your "performance" at the meal. After it was over and you were safely away from the eating area you could relax and refocus on your opponent.

The First Varsity Jersey

Eight grade, 1966, Sulligent, Alabama. Although I was born in Montgomery, Alabama, and lived in Birmingham, Alabama for a while, I do not remember anything other than life as a child I Sulligent. The life I wanted was that of a football player. I had started playing football I the sixth grade. No, it wasn't on the local Toy Bowl or Pee Wee team. They did not have them in Sulligent at the time. It was on the Junior High (7th-9th grades) team. I was able to convince the coaches that I knew what I was getting into and that I would not quit or waste their time. So, my football career began in the 6th grade.

Two years later I was still a boy among what I considered men. I could not wait any longer. I had to be a part of Friday nights. I knew I would not be starting. I really did not think I would be on the field on Friday nights (boy, was I wrong). I would still be playing junior high games, but I would be practicing on a daily basis with the "big boys"! I was excited, but I also knew my place. My place was to do the best I could while learning from the best. Making the decision to join this team instead of just practicing with the junior high team probably had the single biggest impact on my playing career.

After a couple weeks (in the 60's high school were allowed 6 weeks of practice before the first game) of practicing in shorts and helmets it was time for full scale contact. That meant complete uniforms. This particular year Sulligent had practice jerseys with numbers on them. The practice number was also going to be your game number. As I waited in the back of the line, mostly looking straight ahead, I was filled with anticipation as to what number I would "be". You see, you were a number. Not in the sense of just another number, but a number that you would be known as when people watched you, talked about you, in your community or in other towns. Your number often came before your name until, and if, you became good enough for people to say your name instead of your number. We received shoulder pads, pants, knee pads, hip pads, all that was necessary to be prepared for the vicious contact that would soon be coming. However, the most important piece lay ahead. Ass I watched and inched forward, my heart was beating faster, my mouth getting dryer. Then it was handed to me – 64. My thought was, "I'm 64. I will be "64" the next 5 years. I have an identity. Not a number, an identity". I can still visualize it as if it were happening right now. I don't recall the first time I put a game jersey on. For whatever reason, the practice jersey, with a number, meant so much more.

My first high school jersey in the eighth grade and my Senior college jersey.

Standing just to the right of number 24, I'm about to go into the varsity game as an eighth grader.

Football Victory Lines

Every level of football has something special about it. The NFL has a nationwide appeal and is slowly growing into an international sport. In my opinion the international aspect is being forced by the NFL in an ongoing effort to increase revenue, as if they aren't making enough now. College football probably has the most passion among fans. It is often marked by "bandwagon" fans, that every 5 years or so "switch teams", as a new, dominant university rises. Part of the appeal of college football is that most of its fans never attended the particular university that they cheer for but are still all about "we'. High school football is about Friday night lights, pep rallies, local rivalries, being associated with the

High school football has many traditions, but one has almost faded away. One that excited every player who experienced it and every non player that was part of it. It was the pre-kickoff "victory lines". After a team had finished pre-game warmups, they would go back into their field house for a brief period before returning to the field and start play. During this time, the high school band would come on the field, divided in two lines, with a width of about 20 feet between each line. They would start these lines somewhere around the goal line of the end zone closest to where the team had assembled. At this point, the local PA announcer would offer the invitation to "come join the band and make a great Victory Line to help "fire-up" the boys"! This would result I mostly other students, of all ages, not associated with the band or football team, coming onto the field, and extending the lines started by the band. The length of the lines was often determined by the current success of the football team. The greater the success, the longer the lines. Of course, the opposite was also true. The cheerleaders would be I the middle of the lines waiting for the team to run through a sign that they had made and was now being held up by volunteers. This sign always had a clever saying, like "Bump the Bears", "Sting the Jackets", "Tame the Tigers", etc. Sayings that would really inspire 15–17-year-olds! As game time approached, the team would come out of the assembled area, to the field and get right behind the sign. On cue, the band would start playing, the cheerleaders would start running, and the football team would run through the sign and eventually to their sideline. Usually, Seniors were the first to run through the sign as underclassmen dreamed of the day when they would tear into the paper, hearing the ripping sign, and striking fear into the opponent.

Yes, bands are still on the field and cheerleaders still lead the team, but the participation by fans in the lines has gone away. It's sad because a lot of excitement often was associated with coming out of the stands on to the field, being “part” of something, close to the players, band, and cheerleaders and then returning to the stands feeling as you had contributed to what was hopefully going to be a victory. Often, if the game was a big rival, or if the game had more significance than normal, part of the push for the victory lines was for the schools to try and outdo each other with the number of participants. A longer line meant that you “cared” more about your team than did the other school.

A place in the coal mining area of Alabama, Cordova, had a very special twist to the “Victory Line”. There was not a band on the field. There were not any students on the field. The cheerleaders were there but the line was made up of men! When I say men, I mean males that were out of school, ages 20-60, most had played football there or had sons on the team, or just had supported the team for years. These men were SERIOUS. They were not saying, “do the best you can”, “give it your best shot”, or other typical encouraging phrases. They were saying, often mixed with profanity to some degree. “You better make us proud”, “do not let down our community”, “you better not embarrass us”, and so on. They were carrying on a tradition that they had been a part of when they played, and it meant a lot to them. The three years I coached there I was always in awe of this. I had great respect for these elders to be so involved with the young boys on the team. They would back these “demands” with their money and labor if called upon. They were not doing it to draw attention to them but trying to help Cordova continue their winning tradition. I believe it did help with the intensity level of the team because it is one thing for boys to run through a line made up of their peers and another thing to run through a line made up of hard core, no nonsense, men, with high expectations of you.

I don’t know if this tradition still exists in Cordova. I don’t know why the victory line faded away. I loved being in one when I was small, and I enjoyed running through them when I played. It may have become “uncool” to be part of it. It may have had to do with safety issues. It was nice while it lasted.

Integration at SHS

With the start of the 1968 school year Sulligent High School, like every other year, would have some new students. What was different about this year was that two of the new students were African American young men, John, and Olan Truelove. They were soft spoken young men, cousins, who would set several firsts that year. Since they were Seniors, they would be the first Blacks to receive diplomas from SHS and they would be the first Black athletes, as both would play basketball and Olan would play baseball. In spring of 1969 the sport of baseball would return to SHS after an absence of three years because a new gym had been built on the baseball field. In 1969 we still did not have a field and played all our games on the road. I still have a vivid memory of Olan throwing a perfect strike to me from right field, from a good distance and in the air, no hops, to retire a running trying to score what would have been the tying run. I am sure that they endured some verbal abuse. I know that they did not receive any verbal abuse from other baseball players or basketball players because our coach for both sports, Dabbs Earnest, would not permit it, but since they were two grades ahead of me, I do not know what went on in the classrooms, but only one of them was in a fight, once. They were well liked by most of the other students.

I do not know if the Trueloves were a way to get all the White students at Sulligent to get used to integration but the process of complete integration in Lamar County was taking place and most of the community did not know about it. Lamar County, in 1969 had five high schools. Lamar County High School, Kennedy High School, Millport High School, Sulligent High School and Todd High School. All the Black children in the county went to Todd High School. Todd High School was permanently closed after the end of the 1968-69 school year. All Black students would now go to the other four high schools that were closest to their homes.

In 1969 high schools did not have off season or summer workouts. Football players were not around each other unless they played summer league baseball. However, official football practice would start July 15th, which is almost the middle of the summer break between school years at that time. You would meet on that day, have a short "physical" (about ten minutes long per player), go out and start practice in shorts and helmets. A player had better be doing some running on his own during the summer because there was no such thing as easing into practice.

Since there was not any great method of mass communication in 1969, we were told before we had gotten out of school in the spring, what date, what location, and what time to be for football practice to start. About one hour before the designated time to meet the coaches, players started gathering. The White players were gathering on what was at the time a tennis court and the Black players were gathering across the street in front of the high school. There were about 25 White players and about 13 Black players. Instead of the loud, rambunctious activity that boys would be involved in on such a day as this, most of the talk was in small groups, subtle, filled with wonder, questions, anxiety, and nervousness. The Black players were acting the same way. We had not been "counseled" by our coaches as they just expected us as to do the right thing.

About ten minutes before the meeting time, I said to the other White players, "lets go" and started walking toward the Black players. Most of the Black players had a look on their face that said they did not have ayn idea of what was about to happen but were prepared for the worst. I went to the biggest of the Black players and extended my hand and said, "welcome". With that short and simple statement everyone felt much more at ease and most of the players, White and Black, started having small conversations. I was a Junior and during that year and the following year, we never had any type of racial incident, not only on the football team, but all sports and in the hallways and classrooms. It was a peaceful and successful transition to a new way of life.

The Black player who I had approached was Randy Johnson. He was 6'5" and weighed 225. That was a huge player in 1969 and especially for a player who would be a running back for the Blue Devils. Randy and I would have a good relationship at school and afterwards. Randy and I would be invited by the Crimson Tide to visit one of their home games and he had the chance of being one of the first Black players signed by Alabama, but he had hurt his knee enough that even through it did not require surgery, they did not offer him a scholarship. Randy was also a great basketball player, but unfortunately, for me and the Blue Devil program he was a Senior and would only spend one year before graduating. Randy had two sons; both were outstanding athletes. His youngest son, Rashad Johnson, would walk-on at Alabama and not only be able to make the team, he also earned a scholarship, become All-SEC as a Free Safety, and spent several years in the NFL.

As the years passed Sulligent would produce several great athletes, most of them were football players, and a lot of them were Black players. As I would later become a high school coach, I had the opportunity to help some of these players. I was coaching at another school when Tony Truelove was playing at Sulligent. Tony had received very little interest from colleges, but I knew he had talent. I took him and another player from Sulligent to visit Livingston University (West Alabama today). I told them to bring film of the two best games that they would want the Tiger coaches to see. While the players, myself and a Tiger coach toured the campus and had lunch, other Tiger coaches were evaluating the film to determine if they felt either player could contribute.

After lunch the coaches meet privately with both players. Unfortunately for the other player he did not receive a scholarship but was offered to walk-on if he wanted to. However, Tony headed home with a full scholarship in hand! It was an exciting day for Tony and me.

Tony finished his college career as the Tigers fifth all-time leading rusher. He would go on to play with the Minnesota Vikings for a year and a year with the Hamilton Tiger Cats of the CFL. It all started with that long trip in the middle of the spring just weeks before Tony was about to graduate from high school.

Glady Joe Hollis was another great Black football player from Sulligent. Although I did help some in his recruitment by Livingston University, I was more involved with him in a need he had after his Senior season. Glady Joe had led the Tigers in receiving for three straight seasons. He was 6'3" tall and ran a 4.5. forty-yard dash. He had not been drafted but had received a free agent offer from the Buffalo Bills. He asked me to be his agent for the process of negotiating a contract. I was very excited to help! The communication with the Bills, with him, and with me, took a couple of weeks before he signed. I did not ask for any money. I was just happy to see a person from Sulligent achieve success. Although, Glady Joe had a good camp he was cut by the Bills on their final cut before the roster was set.

Integration was good for Sulligent, the school, the community, the White students, the Black students and for society.

N... Lover

Although integration went smoothly at Sulligent there were some racial issues over the years there just like there where in all parts of the country. None were like the violence in Boston or Oxford or Los Angeles, etc., but it did rear its ugly head at times.

In 1985 I had accepted the position of head football coach at Sulligent High School, my alma mater. I had not done my due diligence in researching the entire situation at the time concerning all aspects of what was going on in the community, the football program, the atmosphere at the school, and as it would turn out the dissension between most of the faculty in the county system and the superintendent. I am not going to go into detail about the situation, but the superintendent was very demanding, overly demanding. He was paranoid and power hungry. He had also just been defeated in the election for superintendent and was trying any way he could to become the principal of Sulligent, a position he had held before he became superintendent.

Out of nowhere he called me one day and wanted me to take a day off and drive with him to meet another coach that lived in Georgia. This coach was also from the Sulligent area, but not from Sulligent. He picked me up, we drove to meet this coach, who was surprised when we showed up. The superintendent did a lot of talking with this coach, about an hour, while I did a lot of listening.

We got back in his car and headed back home. On the way back we stopped in Birmingham, and he treated me to a steak dinner. We talked about a lot of things, but he never came to the point about what the trip was really about.

A few weeks later he called me again and wanted me to drive to Sulligent and meet with him and one of the BOE members. We just drove around in his car for almost two hours talking about more specific things which included the head football position at Sulligent High School. Finally, they said, "do you want to be the head football coach at Sulligent?" I was thinking that this was going to happen, but it was certainly not happening the way of hiring a football coach was normally done.

First, the head football coach and his assistant at Sulligent had not resigned or had their positions terminated. The Superintendent assured me that this was not a big deal. I would later figure out that I had been a pawn in a scheme by the superintendent to get his position as principal of Sulligent High School back. The football program at Sulligent had not been successful for the last couple of years so he thought that if he brought in someone new, he would get a lot of credit and the community would push for his return as principal. That did not happen. Evidently, his actions as superintendent over the previous four years had led to his opposition, not only throughout the county, but even more so in Sulligent.

He did get the BOE to hire me, even through the other two coaches were still part of the school system, but he was not hired as principal. Now I was in a situation in which the new superintendent thought I was a big supporter of the old superintendent, a new principal that had never been in administration, inheriting a football team that I was not able to go through spring practice with and would only have four weeks to put in my system before the first game, and a student body that was not used to discipline for the past few years. I learned a big lesson from this experience.

The football season was not going well, but the part I want to focus on has to deal with racism. Most of the people in Sulligent were good people but there were a handful who felt entitled for whatever reason and that they thought their child should receive special treatment. These 5-6 families were all White. I had replaced a White quarterback with a Black player and had moved a White defensive player from his usual position to another position and replaced him with a Black player. Both moves were an attempt to improve the team, but as I had told the team they were not permanent moves and competition and performance during practice and games could result in other changes.

During the last few weeks of the season one of my friends said he needed to meet me at the school. I told him to come after practice. When he arrived, he was very somber, like he had some news he knew he had to tell me but did not want to. He said, "I found these around town last night". What he found were signs written on printer paper. The message on them, "**JERRY PITTS IS A N….. LOVER!"**

Stunned. Disbelief. Sad. Defeated. These were some of the emotions that went through me as I read them. However, anger was not one of them. He had collected about a dozen of them. We both knew who were involved in writing and dispersing them throughout the town. I did not immediately approach them but waited for the most opportune time to embarrass them. That would come later at a meeting of several parents, most of them involved in the signs were there along with several parents that supported me. At an appropriate time during the meeting, I pulled out the signs and showed them for all to see. Many of those in attendance seen them for the first time and were shocked. Those responsible were caught off guard and showed physical signs of anxiety and nervousness. I did not call out any names because I did not have any physical evidence to point to those responsible, but instead I said, " those responsible for these have low self-esteem, are racists who only want their purposes meet not what is best for the team, are cowards who work in the middle of the night, who would want to sow discord instead of togetherness, and who are full of false pride". That ended the meeting.

No one ever came worth to admit what they did or to apologize. I never expected anyone to because that is how those type of people operate. It did not affect any of my coaching decisions as I was true to myself.

362

As I started my Senior in high school, I was looking forward to what I was hoping would be the greatest year of my life to that point. I would not be disappointed. I had several great friends, the football, basketball, and baseball teams that I was a part of had a lot of talent and we were anxious for those seasons. I was about to turn 18, was in great physical shape, and there was very little for me to be concerned about.

The involvement of the United States in the Vietnam War had been going for several years without any progress. I was a big supporter of the United States being in Viet Nam because we had to stop communism from spreading, even through Viet Nam was a very small country on the other side of the world, that if communism overtook Viet Nam all of Asia and then Australia and New Zealand would be next. At least that is what most of us were told and believed. However, I was a Senior and the nightly news reports about the war did not really sink in as long as more Viet Cong were killed that day that U. S. soldiers. I did not have a good concept about what was going on in Viet Nam.

Looking back the administrations that got the United States involved in the Viet Nam war and the administrations that kept us there, before President Nixon put an end to it, were completely wrong. It was a conflict we should never have been a part of. Those politicians should have learned some lessons form the Korean War. The United States had never fought a war in the jungle, and they greatly underestimated the will of the Vietnam people to keep foreigners out of their country and had overestimated the threat of communism to that part of the world. However, I greatly salute and honor all the military men and women who served in that war.

Football season passed. We had gone 9-2-1 and made it to the semifinals of the playoffs. Basketball season passed and although we had to replace four starters from the previous season, we had gone 16-12. Baseball season had passed, and we had gone 16-2 with only 2 losses coming in the finals of the state championship. Graduation had passed. The Vietnam War was still going strong with no end in sight.

The first of June I was facing several realities. My life was about to completely change since high school was in the past. I would soon be out of my home, and not just for a weekend visit somewhere. I was going to a college to play football, but since it was not Auburn, I was not very excited about that. I was also facing the military draft.

By 1971 the draft was a very political issue. Accusations about some getting preferential treatment and not getting drafted while others had to go into the military were rampant. Young men were leaving the country to not have to face being drafted. So, the draft process was changed. A lottery was now being used. The process would be televised. There would be a huge cylinder with 366 blue capsule balls. On the inside of the capsule was a date. The balls would be drawn one at a time. Whatever date that was on the inside of the capsule would be assigned to whatever number capsule that was drawn. For example, if the date inside the first capsule was April 10, those born on April 10 would be the first ones drafted. If the second capsule drawn was February 23, then those born on that date would be the second ones drafted. This went on until all of the capsules had been drawn and each date had a number. The lower the number the higher the chance a person would be drafted.

By the time I had graduated from high school I had a much more serious outlook toward Viet Nam. I had realized that those totals on the nightly news were real deaths and not a sporting event scoreboard. I had also known of one person from Sulligent who had been killed by a sniper. Things were getting real. I was not going to join the military, but I knew that I would go if drafted.

I had one final sporting event to participate in before going to college. It was the Alabama High School Athletic Association All-Star football game. It was in Tuscaloosa and played in Denny stadium on the campus of the University of Alabama. It was still Denny stadium at the time as it had not yet been named after Bear Bryant. We practiced on the Crimson Tide's practice field and stayed in the dorms on campus. There was not any social media, IPhones, or such, and long-distance telephone calls were expensive. We had 7-10 days to practice before the game. I cannot remember the exact number. Almost every day we had two practices. My day consisted of eating breakfast, practicing, eating lunch, resting, practicing again, eating dinner, then going to my room and resting. This was in July. It was also during the time that the draft lottery would take place for that calendar year.

The night of the draft I went to my room knowing that my future and my life could be completely changed when I woke up. I was too tired to stay up and watch it on television and I knew that watching it was not going to change the outcome.

The next morning after getting up, I headed to breakfast. As I came into the dorm lobby, I noticed a newspaper lying on one of the tables. I paused and stared at it for a few seconds. I then said in my mind that nothing is going to change, go look at the paper. My birthday is December

10. The number that was drawn for December 9 was 24. The number drawn for December 11 was 36.

The Number Drawn For December 10 Was 362!

It took me a few seconds for it to soak in what I was looking at. I finally realized that almost every other young man in the United States would be drafted before I would be. I tossed the paper back on the table, headed to breakfast, and was looking forward to a grueling practice in the oppressive heat of summer against other physical and talented football players! I know a blessing when I see one.

Olivia

"Grease"! What is the first thing that pops into your mind! Either John Travolta or Olivia Newton-John. Livingston University, with its limited resources still tried to give the student body some quality entertainment throughout the year in the form of 3 to 4 concerts. In 1975 they gave us probably what is still to this day one of, if not the top, performer to ever visit the campus. Plus, all the concerts were free to the students.

They gave us Olivia Newton-John.

Olivia had become a superstar in 1975 with an album and several top hits like, "I Honestly Love You", "Let Me BE There", and "If You Love Me Let Me Know", just to name a few.

Olivia was coming to Livingston.

Then a rumor started going around the campus. Olivia had become a millionaire almost overnight and Livingston had a contract with her that would pay her $25,000. Now, to me, $25,000 would be a good day's pay and even more so for about an hour and a half of work. However, she was in great demand and could easily afford to pay whatever amount it would be for her to cancel the concert. Most of the student body was hopeful that she would still come, but most were also resigned to accepting the possibility that she wouldn't. She did not have any ties to anyone in Alabama, much less the small town of Livingston. It would not even be a blimp on her skyrocketing career if she did not come.

I am still not sure why she came. I like to think it had to do with character, keeping a person's word, and maybe even about remembering where she had been before her giant breakthrough.

She played to an audience of around 2,000. She put as much into her performance as if she were in some major city in front of 20,000 people. She performed for an hour and a half, singing all her hits, and acting like there was not anywhere else in the world she wanted to be at that time other than Livingston University.

Thank You Olivia.

“Jerry Pitts Field”

“No one player is bigger than the team”. Fortunately, all my coaches in high school and college believed this and it carried over into my coaching philosophy. This is a story about teamwork, desire, dedication, passion, and compassion. This is a story about a community coming together to achieve something most people would have said was impossible.

In the spring and summer of 1966, a beautiful new basketball gymnasium had been built for Sulligent High School. The days of playing in the high school auditorium was over. It was not a renovation and everything about it either shined or smelled good or just felt “strong”. Everyone was proud of it. The only negative niche about it was that because of the need to be close to the rest of the high school buildings it had been built on the infield of the existing baseball field. The baseball program had come to a screeching halt!

Finally, in the spring of 1970 the Town of Sulligent received a grant to build a new baseball facility. The groundwork was done by the local National Guard before the contractor came in to build the dugouts, press box, to put up the fencing and to install the lights. Sulligent instantly had one of the best fields in the area. There were a couple of drawbacks. It did not have a grass infield, which almost none of the fields in that era did, and the dirt in the infield contained locks of pebbles, heck, lets just call it what it really was, rocks. That did not matter to us the players. We had a home field!

Play on the new field started with a few games that summer. The first official season would be the following 1971 season. However, something that had not happened in the previous two seasons of playing baseball on the road happened at the new field – HOMERUNS! In fact, I would hit the first home run ever hit by a Blue Devil or an opponent in the stadium. The first one I hit felt surreal. I did not realize it had gone over until after rounding first base. Then with a grin from ear to ear I kept running around the bases, unimpeded, until I touched home plate. I would hit four homeruns that summer including one game in which I had two 3-run homeruns. They all felt great, and it also felt great to watch my teammates hit homeruns.

We were now able to take batting practice without having to chase every foul ball or missed ball. We had fencing! We became better defensively as we could do as much defensive work as we needed. They were one caveat. All the infielders would take a few moments before every practice and game to pick up and throw over the fence excessive size pebbles and the other players would do the same to the sliding areas at second and third base and at home plate. This helped to an extent but there were still some bad bounces on ground balls and some pain associated with sliding.

In the spring of 1971, the new field would be christened with its first official season, and what a season it was. With five seniors, led by Kenneth Humbers right arm and his bat, the Blue Devils put together a magical season. The seniors included Humbers who also played third base, me at catcher, Jimmy Ray at first base who was also our second pitcher, Mike Knight at second base, and Carlos Flynn at shortstop. Every senior had their best year of their career. Kenneth was 10-1 as a pitcher. He could bring the heat but also had a curveball that seemed like it broke a mile. It was a pleasure catching him. He also led the team with a .418 batting average, in hits, doubles, and total bases. He also was tied for the most RBIs, and home runs. The five seniors had a combined batting average of .358. I also hit the first grand slam in the new stadium.

Baseball had a much shorter season in that era than now. Everyone had to wait until spring training football was over to start playing baseball. That meant a team would only play a few games before the area games and playoffs would start. We were 13-0 when Autaugaville came into town to play us for the state championship. The fact is they had more talent than us and we came in second place. It was not what we wanted but more than we dreamed about before the season started.

However, our season was not over. The 8 schools in that area had formed what was called the West Alabama Conference. They would compete for a championship in football, basketball, and baseball. Since the concept of state championships in baseball was relatively new and there were few local teams making the playoffs, the conference championship always ended the season. None of us wanted to end the season, much less with two disappointing loses, so we decided to play in it. We swept three games to win the championship and finish the season at 16-2. Although we had had some success the previous two seasons when playing all our games on the road, we certainly benefited by having a home field.

As time passed and I went to college and started my coaching career, Sulligent would have up and down seasons in baseball as far as success was concerned. They would win area championships from time to time but not make any noise in the playoffs. The baseball facility itself was becoming in disrepair.

After the 1993-94 school year ended, I had just completed my second year at South Lamar High School. South Lamar was a consolidated school in the same county as Sulligent, about 25 miles apart. I was the defensive coordinator for the football team, head girls' basketball coach, and head baseball coach. I had been there two years and the baseball team had gone to the state playoffs each year. I had two men approach me about being the baseball coach for Sulligent. Both men, Danny Hollis and Alan Weeks had sons in the program and Weeks was over the recreational department for the city. An attempt for me to come to Sulligent had been made the year before, but it was not feasible. Besides I was enjoying my time as a Stallion. However, they held an ACE that tugged on my heart so much that I told them I would come. My son, Nathan, was at Sulligent. He would be a sophomore. I had been able to see him play a little bit while being in the same county but now I would be able to coach him. Although this made it an easy decision, I also knew that I was giving up being defensive coordinator for the football team which had the potential to win the state championship (they would finish third) and to coach a baseball team that was loaded with talent. On the Sulligent end, I would be an assistant coach on the football but would be standing around most of the time as the head coach did not delegate any real responsibility to his assistants in any of aspect of the game. I would also be inheriting a baseball program that had won 3 games total over the previous two seasons. I would also be inheriting a facility that had become a danger to be around, much less play on. The four-foot-high side fences were bent from people leaning on them and in parts the fence was not up. After over twenty years of little maintenance the outfield fence was not much better and had several holes at the bottom of it. The press box needed work and the bathrooms inside it stank. The dugouts had slats in the front and sides instead of being fully covered. And yes, there were still rocks on the infield.

In 1971 the town of Sulligent had received a grant to build this field. In 1994 this would turn out to be a blessing for me as I, with the help of many parents and boosters, would attempt to create a first-class winning program. Since the town owned the field, they were responsible for maintaining it. They would have more resources to make improvements than if the local school system owned it. Plus, improving a baseball field would be a low priority for a school system that did not have much local tax money coming into it.

The two men I previously mentioned, along with my daddy Leon Pitts, and me met a couple of times to discuss the future of the baseball program. I told them the first step to being successful was that the players had to believe that the program meant something to them by the actions of the boosters and parents. We wanted a winning program not just a "team". I told them if they fixed the stadium, I would do my part in preparing the players to play winning baseball. They agreed.

Although Sulligent had only won three games in two seasons, I could tell they had some young talent and a couple of talented seniors, that if they all pulled the same way could be successful. I was able to be confirmed as the new baseball coach before the summer league season started. This was a vital step in winning. Most schools take the summer league with a ho-hum, relaxed attitude. I knew I could not do that. I had to immediately establish rules and change or improve attitudes. I had to make the players understand that if they were not going to do what I asked, when I asked it, and how I asked it that I did not want them around. The only questions I wanted asked was if it was about how to improve a technique. It was either a complete buy-in or bye.

We had a few days practice before the first summer league game. Those practices were well organized and intense without much fun. I went around the stations watching with a snarl on my face. I did not want to be anyone's friend, I wanted to be their coach. I dressed in appropriate coaching attire every day, and we established some rules and made some necessary changes immediately. Since South Lamar was in the same area as Sulligent, I had played against the Blue Devils twice each season the two previous seasons. Although I did see some talent, I also noticed a lot of bad habits that needed correcting. No caps turned backwards, shirts tucked in, being dressed before you came into the dugout or on the field, when you moved you ran, helping with equipment and field preparation, proper stretching before throwing, running foul poles, and being on time. These rules were established immediately, other rules would follow. This approached paid off. I knew we had to experiencing winning no matter if it was summer league or not. They were going through the hard work, but the feel of winning would only enforce that work and habits when next spring rolled around. We went 11-6 that summer and when it ended, I knew, and the players believed that we could win on a consistent basis. Excitement was high for the baseball program among the players, parents, and boosters.

The players and me had done our part. It was time for the others to do theirs. And they did. The Saturday after the last game on the previous Thursday there were about 15 men at the baseball facility at 8 a.m. They were there to lay sod on the infield. After a few hours it was laid, and we turned the water on it. It was an amazing event to see grass covering the infield that had gone 24 years without it. The following week my father secured two $1,000 donations which would be used to build new dugouts. Shortly after that the old dugouts were demolished, new concrete pads were poured and the new dugouts, which were about twice as big as the old, were built mostly with free labor including my father and uncle, Lamar Pitts. This was before school started that fall. The next January the city paid for a new backstop, which was about three times as big as the old backstop and fencing down each side. I insisted that the fencing down each side be six feet tall to prevent spectators from leaning on it. I also insisted that gates that would let players into the field be 15 feet from the end of the dugouts. This would prevent parents, which had been a problem at Sulligent, from leaning in and asking their child if they needed anything or to complain about playing time. I needed focus and this was one way it was achieved.

We had a great attitude as a team after winning during the summer and having a much-improved facility. In 1995 we went 12-11. We won the area championship, mainly by beating South Lamar twice, and won the first-round state playoff game which was played at Sulligent. In the past, because of size dimension rules, if the baseball facility had not been improved the Blue Devils would not have been allowed to host a playoff game.

More improvements, and more importantly more wins would come. Over the next ten years some of the improvements would be an expanded outfield which also leveled the field as it had had a slight dip, a warning track, a new outfield fence that was eight foot high except in the middle 150 feet as it was 15 feet high, and it was covered with a rubber like substance. A new nine inning scoreboard. Two new high rise aluminum bleachers, press box and rest room renovations. Concrete sidewalks. Creating a bull pen area on the home side. New light poles and lights. Putting pure dirt on the infield running/fielding area which eliminated rocks. Other improvements continued after I left including a large dressing room attached to the first base side dugout. We also had the best PA announcer in Booty Morris. Not only could he announce the lineups and give the name of each batter as they came to bat, but he entertained the crowd with good music, trivia, and witty comments. These improvements were because of a community that loved their kids and loved baseball. Parents and boosters came and went, but there was always another group ready to take their place. Mostly, I just gave a vision and asked for it to be fulfilled and in almost every case it was. I was blessed to be around what was mostly selfless people.

The wins came too. In the 11 years that I was the head coach the Blue Devils won 191 games, went to the State Playoffs 10 times and finished State AAA runner-up in 2001. Several players signed college scholarships to play baseball and one, Eric Hollis, signed with the Chicago White Sox, and made it to their AA franchise in Birmingham.

I was just a cog in a big wheel that produced some good times on the diamond.

My father died in February of 2003. He was at almost every game I coached during those 11 years. He would miss some road games, but not many. He even traveled with us on a few of the playoff games in which an overnight stay was needed. The players loved him, and them, along with their parents and boosters bought, paid for, and put a plaque up on the press box honoring his devotion to the baseball teams.

Close to the end of the 2004 season we were having one of the best seasons ever at Sulligent. We were in the middle of what would be a 21-game winning streak on the way to the area championship and another state playoff competition. After most games the players help to quickly work on the field, put up equipment and leave expect for the pitchers who must do some running. I never had long meetings after games, win or lose. I wanted to take time to evaluate the game in my mind and discuss it more with the team the next day. However, after this game I noticed a lot of the fans and nearly all the players were just kind of standing around, mingling, and there was a kind of quiet among them. Suddenly, I see some of the players carrying two sheets of metal toward the scoreboard but there was not any writing on them. Then Booty Morris starts talking on the PA. He sounds official and starts reading a proclamation. The proclamation says that the City of Sulligent has officially named the baseball field "Jerry Pitts Field". As soon as he finishes his talk, the players turn the metal around and it is blue with white letters that spell out Jerry Pitts Field. This had all been done with complete secrecy toward me. Never had I expected such an honor. I was so humbled that I almost went to my knees. I was speechless as parents and players came by to congratulate me. They were all happy for me, but I could hardly respond. I do not take this honor lightly as it is probably the most touching recognition that I ever received.

In my heart I know this should have been named something like "Community Field", because no one person is bigger than the team, but because of their love of the game and the love for their sons playing the game, it had resulted in what had transpired over the last decade. I will always cherish the honor and more importantly the players, parents, and boosters that made it possible.

IN
MEMORY
OF
LEON PITTS
FOR YEARS OF
DEDICATION
AND
SUPPORT

My Best Friend

Leslie, My Wife

My All-Time Favorite Player

My Son, Nathan

Pitts named to 3-A All State Academic Baseball Team

Nathan Pitts, a 1997 graduate of Sulligent High School was recently named to the Birmingham News Class 3-A All State Academic Baseball Team. Pitts finished the year with a 4.00 grade point average. Nathan is the son of Julia Gooch and Jerry Pitts of Sulligent. In the photo, SHS Coach, Jerry Pitts congratulates Nathan for being named to the All State Team.

My Favorite Ball Girl

My Daughter, Ashley

Whatever It Takes to Make the Field Better

JERRY PITTS FIELD
Enjoy Coca-Cola
POWERADE
AT BAT
BALL
STRIKE
OUT
H/E
GUEST
HOME
1 2 3 4 5 6 7 8 9 10 RUNS HITS ERR

Chapter 5

The Wheels on the Bus Go Round and Round

A school bus looks innocent, but believe me, it is full of Gremlins

The Wheels On The Bus Go Round And Round

When I was in high school the only team to travel by bus for sporting competitions was the football team. There were not any girl's teams in any sports at the time. The basketball and baseball teams traveled in personal cars. Each coach drove a car with as many players as possible and then the older players who had a car and who had parents that would let them drive to competitions would take the remaining players. No one complained when driving, because like all teenagers, we loved the opportunity to drive, It also gave us a sense of being needed more than just as a player. A player who drove his car was never reimbursed for gas. It never crossed anyone's mind to ask for the school to put gas into our car or give us money. Finances were tight in those days. The concept of booster clubs and fund raisers was a novelty. The first booster club that Sulligent formed at the beginning of my sophomore year, and it focused only on the football team. A nice reward for traveling by car was that if you were not in a car on a coach you could listen to music and talk about anything you wanted to. When traveling by bus, or in a car with a coach, the moment you set foot on the bus or in the car, you were silent for the entire trip. The only time you spoke was if you were asked a question by a coach. However, if the team was successful in whatever competition that they were in, everyone talked freely on the return trip. Losing meant silence.

It was several years into my coaching career before every team from every sport traveled by bus to every competition. Girls were now competing in basketball and softball, so the number of overall athletes had greatly increased. However, the biggest factor that caused schools to switch to using buses all the time to transport athletes was liability. At some point in time the administrations of schools across the state realized that they were just as responsible for students in after school events as they were in a school day, on-campus setting. Whereas a school would be covered by insurance if something happened with a student being transported on a school owned bus, they would be without any protection if something happened if a student were driving their personal vehicle, even by themselves.

Most coaches did not have licenses to drive buses. That meant that a licensed bus driver would have to be secured and that that person would have to be paid. Most of these drivers were people who had a regular, daily, bus route for the school. Finding a driver like this was usually not a problem for the football or basketball teams. Those teams usually would depart for their destinations a few hours after the school day had ended, which gave drivers who had daily, regular routes to be able to return to school in plenty of time to transport the football or basketball teams.

This was not the case for baseball or softball. Most competitions involving these sports would start around 4 p.m. This put a hardship on finding someone who could leave during the school day. If it was a regular driver the school had to find a substitute driver for that person's route. There were substitute drivers available but not all of them were sports fans and would not drive. Some years I was lucky to find that one person who had a license and who loved baseball. Some years it was a struggle to find a driver every time a road game was scheduled.

Finally, I decided to take matters into my own hands. I decided to get my license to drive a bus. This would not be as easy it one might think. The first step was to get my CDL, commercial drivers license. A person would need to already have a regular drivers license. You would then go to the DMV to take four different written tests. I had gathered study materials for each different test, put time into studying them, and went to take the tests. CDL is used mostly by drivers who drive the 18 wheelers. It does cover some smaller vehicles but there is a state law that to drive the big yellow bus you must have a CDL. Every test went well except one. The test was about brakes. This was a new concept for me in that I did not have any practical experience with air brakes or other braking issues on vehicles other than passenger cars and trucks. I passed the test with a score that was exactly on the pass/fail number. Good enough for me!

The next step was to learn how to drive a school bus. An average school bus is around 11 feet high. 35 to 40 feet long, about 8 feet wide and weighs abound 24,000 pounds. It is one of the safest methods of transportation available. It has been a bright yellow for a long time, but newer buses have reflective striping, better warning light systems, and overall better visibility. They all have power steering and air brakes. Many school systems are replacing old buses with those that have air conditioning systems in them. All buses now have automatic transmissions which allow the driver to keep both hands on the steering wheel. Some buses are now equipped where almost all necessary functions for the bus to operate properly, such as opening and closing the door, turning warning lights on and off, built into the steering wheel, again allowing the driver to keep both hands on the steering wheel. Oversized front windows and larger mirrors allow drivers to see their surroundings better. Seats for the students are high enough that in the unlikely event of a crash they would not go forward over the seat. Seatbelts are not provided on most buses and in my opinion, this is a good thing. Most students who ride school buses are elementary students, these students would be at a higher risk of danger should they be buckled into their seats with seatbelts and an emergency situation should occur, such as a bus fire, and require a quick evacuation. Panic could set in among the younger students and they might not be able to exit the bus. A bed of a school bus also sits higher than that of most passenger cars. They are made of steel and in almost all instances, a car that hits a bus is going to have much more damage than the bus. The school bus is safe and becoming safer all the time.

The first step in getting a bus driving license is not getting behind the wheel and practicing driving, backing, and parking. The first step is learning the pre-trip inspection. There are 71 items to go over in a pre-trip inspection. You must be able to touch them or point to them and tell them what their importance is. Most of these items are in and around the engine, but there also cover include items around the wheels and tires, dashboard, and even walking down the aisle on the inside of the bus. Walking down the aisle to the end of the bus is also mandatory after the bus has had students on it to make sure none have fallen asleep and remain on the bus. The best way to learn the pre-trip inspection was to do it on a bus over and over. Since the pre-trip inspection is as much a physical activity as a mental one, practice on a real bus was the only way to prepare.

In my situation, after I had received my CDL, I was given permission to have a licensed bus driver give me driving lessons. In the beginning these lessons were given on school property. Eventually lessons were given on public roads. Since most incidents/accidents with buses that are the fault of the bus driver occur when backing up, this technique was practiced more than anything else. The biggest obstacle to overcome in the beginning was the fact that you had to trust your side mirrors when backing up. The aisle mirror was mostly useless because it did not give you a true picture of your distance and the area you had to back into. Eventually I gave the mirrors my trust and was able to back a bus up as well as I could my car.

The school system would have a once a year "bus school". This was for remediation and updates for veteran drivers and, also the time in which potential new drivers would take their pre-trip inspection test and road test. I was able to pass both and get my license on the first try.

This was a great relief as I was now able to leave with my baseball team at the appropriate time for any scheduled away game. This was one less worry that I would now have on game day. It would also put me on the path to my next goal, having a full-time bus route. A teacher's salary is determined by the college degree that person has plus the number of years of experience. This is the same for everyone. However, there are a lot of extracurricular activities within a school system that must be supervised by an employee of the school system. Most of the time these activities are supervised by teachers. Depending on what the activity is, these teacher's salary is then supplemented by additional income. This income is often based on the financial resources of the individual school system, whereas most of the teaching salary is paid for by the state. This means that a baseball coach in one system could be paid a lot more than a baseball coach in a different system. The reason that one of my goals was to become a bus driver with a daily, regular bus route was that this would pay me about five times as much as the supplement did for me coaching baseball. To achieve this, I had to convince the administration that I was serious about wanting a regular bus route. I would volunteer anytime there was a need for a substitute bus driver on a regular route. It did not matter to me if the route was short or long, I would take it. I eventually received a full-time route, but I had to promise that I would remain as the baseball coach. This was not a problem for me as I was still enjoying coaching baseball very much.

During my years driving a bus on my designated route it was the same routine almost every day. At times, weather conditions would interrupt that routine, but those instances were rare. I became a much better driver of my personal vehicle because of the training and constant awareness one must have to safely transport children on a school bus. However, there were a few instances that are worth recalling. Instances that began badly, but all ended well. The following instances are not in chronological order but in order of from the least interesting to the head scratching ones.

DECEPTION: Every time that I was asked to be a substitute bus driver, other than during baseball season, I said yes. It paid a small sum and if I did enough during a month then it was a nice bump. My main goal was to convince the administration that I was loyal to them, willing to help, that I could handle any route, and that I would be a great candidate for a full-time route if a position ever came open. The biggest problem with driving a substitute route was having a student on board that knew the direction of the route and the starts that needed to be made for students to exit at the proper location. Elementary students were the majority riding a bus. Most of them only knew where to get off the bus and little else about the route. This created some headaches, but fortunately, only a few times did I have to backtrack and let off a student who had missed their stop.

This route was one of my first substitute assignments. It was a bigger bus and probably had about fifty students on it for the afternoon trip. A route was usually designated as a tough route or easy route, not by the length of the route, but by how many times you had to back up and turn around. This route had several back- ups. However, I had come to one that looked so easy. There was not a building right next to it or any trees or ditches. It was flat. Flat can be deceiving. It had rained a good bit the previous two days and although I could see some small water standing it was all flat. I put the bus in reverse, moved backward and everything felt solid. Not one bit of sinking. I put the bus in the drive and no movement occurred. My back tires were literally spinning on flat ground. I learned that day that buses do not have great traction for pushing themselves on wet ground regardless of the elevation. I put the bus in reverse, but it did not move backwards. I put the bus in the drive, but it did not move. One thing that a bus driver never wants to do is exit the bus while students are still on it, but I did not have any choice. There were not any cell phones, so I was on my own. I had two options. One was to sit there and wait until parents started realizing that their babies were not home on time and help would eventually arrive, or two, get off the bus and see what I could do to get unstuck.

Looking at the rear tires I noticed that they had not sunk down into the ground any. There was just spinning on the grass and water. This was good. Before I did the backing and turning, I had let a student off at her house about a tenth of a mile from where we were at. She had become curious and had walked down to see what the problem was. I explained to her that I needed a shovel and anything flat, like plywood or cardboard if they had any. She went to her house and brought back a square shovel and two pieces of short plywood. I made a short trench as wide of the width of the two tires on both sides of the bus and jammed the plywood up under the tires as far as they would go. I gave the shovel back to the girl and told her that I hoped that I would not need it anymore. Getting back on the bus, I started the engine, paused, put the bus in drive and floored the pedal. The bus went across the plywood, and we proceeded on the route. I was muddy, but I was not going to complain at all since I was able to resume the route, and no one needed to know about getting stuck on flat ground.

FUEL GUAGE: To have a successful program on a continuous basis in any sport you must develop your younger players and not just focus totally on your current varsity players. My philosophy was to put focus on winning at the varsity level by playing my best players regardless of their age, race, or who their parents might be, while focusing on developing skills on the junior varsity team with winning being a plus. If we lost a game but got better individually than it was a successful contest. On the junior varsity, everyone played some in every game. I tried to get everyone at least one at bat, but since junior varsity games were only 5 innings long that did not always happen. We would play a junior varsity game almost every time we had a varsity game scheduled. When we were in a tournament, or had a varsity doubleheader scheduled, or if the varsity game were on a weeknight and either team had to travel a long distance, then sometimes there would not be a junior varsity game played. Rarely did the junior varsity play contest when a varsity game was not scheduled. However, this event occurred when the Vernon coach and I had scheduled a junior varsity double header on a weeknight. It was to be played at Vernon.

Vernon is only ten miles from Sulligent. The Bulldogs and Blue Devils have been bitter rivals in all sports since the two schools started playing sports. Although bitter rivals, most of the contests were played with sportsmanship. Since I was only taking the junior varsity on a short trip the administration had asked me to use one of the spare buses so that I would not have to refuel or clean up after the game any of the regular route buses. I had a short practice with the varsity players and then went to the area where the spare buses were parked and found one that had the keys in it. It was one of the few remaining buses that used gasoline instead of diesel. I started the engine and checked the fuel gauge. Over one fourth of a tank of fuel was in the bus, plenty to go to Vernon and back.

It was a great spring night for baseball. Crisp weather but not too cool to enjoy being outside. I do not remember which team won either game, but I remember it being a success since all the junior varsity players got significant playing time and plenty of at-bats. On all travel games I required the players to ride the bus to the games, but if their parents were at the games, they could ride home with them if they wanted to. This usually meant that I would have very few players riding back on the bus after away games. The routine after most away games was to find a place to stop and let the players get something to eat and drink. At some towns fast food establishments were available, at others we would stop at a convenience store. However, since this was a school night, and we were only 10 miles from home I decided just to drive straight back.

Approximately 3 miles from Vernon, heading toward Sulligent, the bus engine started sputtering. I looked at my assistant coach and he said, "it sounds like you are running out of fuel". Well, he was right. The fuel gauge had lied. I pulled the bus onto the shoulder as much as possible. The bus was on a very slight downward and sideward incline. Nothing dangerous as far as the bus moving, but it would be a significant factor later. We were on a four-lane road so that made the situation a lot safer than if we had been on a two-lane road. Again, no cell phones. Fortunately, there were only a few players on the bus. Unfortunately, all the parents that had been at the game had gone on ahead. I was stumped as to what to do. Eventually a young person from Vernon stopped to ask what was wrong. I explained my situation to him and asked if he would be so kind as to take me back to Vernon and let me get some gas. He was glad to help. Vernon had one major convenience store that stayed open most of the night. That is the one we went to. Besides needing gas, I also had two other major problems. I did not have anything to put the gas in and I did not have my billfold or any money.

I still had my baseball uniform on which clearly identified me with Sulligent High School. There were three young workers at the convenience store. I explained the situation to them, told me that I needed a gas can, and about 5 gallons of gas, but that I would have to come back tomorrow and pay for it all. All three of them just stared at me for a few moments before they all just started shaking their heads like I had thrown a ball of confusion bomb into their world. They seemed scared and no was their only answer they had for me. As I tried to explain the situation in further detail, they only dug in their heels deeper. I finally convinced them to call the owner, tell him the situation, and who I was and that I would be back tomorrow to pay for all costs. Fortunately, I did know the owner and he knew me, and I was able to walk out of the store with a new gas can and 5 gallons of gas. The young man drove me back to the bus. Shortly we would be heading on to our destination.

The assistant coach had stayed with the bus and the players and started smiling when I got out of the car with the can of gas. I was smiling too as I told him the difficulty that I had had in obtaining it. The feeling of relief soon vanished. As I went to put the gas into the tank of the bus it would not fit. The bus was sitting at such an angle that the nozzle on the gas can would not go into the tank of the bus so that I could raise the gas can high enough for the gas to go into the tank. Ultimate frustration enveloped us. I let the assistant coach try to get the gas into the tank, but he did not have any better luck than I did. We paused for a moment and just thought. We decided that we had to have some sort of extension to go from the gas can nozzle to the opening of the gas tank on the bus. We looked and the answer we needed was only six feet away from us in the form of a discarded 24-ounce, plastic soda bottle. There was a pair of scissors in the medical kit and I proceeded to cut off the bottom of the bottle and part of the top of the bottle. We stuck the bottle into the opening of the tank on the bus and were able to point it upward. As the assistant coach held the bottle, I was able to slowly pour the gas through the bottle and into the gas tank of the bus.

With everyone back on the bus I put my seatbelt on and had my fingers crossed that the engine would start. Anytime a vehicle runs out of fuel there is a possibility that if you do not have enough fuel in the tank that it will not be pulled up into the engine to start. This was an older bus, and I was nervous that with everything else that had gone wrong that it would not start. However, with the turn of the key the engine started immediately, and we headed to Sulligent. We had plenty of fuel to get to Sulligent and brought to close what should have been a routine trip. After that experience, before every trip I would fuel completely up whatever bus I was going to drive no matter the distance of the trip. And, yes, I did return to Vernon the next day and settle my debt.

SOAKED: My high school coaches and then my college coaches were consistent about one thing, if you were going to travel to a contest your method of travel would leave exactly when they said it would. They were not going to wait on anyone. I accepted this philosophy immediately in my coaching career. This meant that if I were going to enforce this rule then I had to make sure that I was never late in being ready to leave or I could not justify leaving a player who was late.

In this event I was not coaching. I had volunteered to drive the boy's junior varsity basketball team to their destination because on this night they would be playing much earlier than the varsity team would. The varsity basketball head coach will be driving the varsity team later. I had gone home after the school day, relaxed for a while, and then had gotten dressed for the trip. Anytime I represented the school at an event, I would dress in slacks and a polo style shirt, never in blue jeans and such. I left my house 45 minutes before the scheduled departure time for the junior varsity team. I parked my vehicle in the bus parking lot, got onto the bus that had been assigned for the trip and pulled it up to the fuel tank to fuel it up. I had about 35 minutes left before departure time. I was in good shape. They gauge showed that the bus was half full so it would need about twenty to twenty-five gallons of fuel. I put the nozzle into the opening of the gas tank, locked it on the handle and began fueling the bus. While fueling I went back on to the bus, walked the aisle, making sure there was not anything on the bus that was not supposed to be there, like a sleeping child. Everything looked good. By this time, I knew that the fuel tank should be close to being full, so I started down the steps of the bus to exit it.

The fuel tank opening on most school buses is about two feet from the opening of the bus door. At the exact same moment that my second foot touched the ground outside the bus, the fuel pump handle exploded from the opening of the fuel tank and sprayed me with diesel fuel. When the handle hit the ground the lock on the handle disengaged and the fuel stopped coming out. However, I was soaked with diesel fuel from the waist down. What are the odds? Standing there stunned I had several thoughts going on at one time. I now had 25 minutes before departure time. I had two options. I could drive the bus, soaked in diesel fuel, or go back home, change, and come back. Since I was driving these players to an early game, I was also going to have to supervise them as an administrator until the principal arrived later. This did not seem like a good option. However, if I went home there would be a good possibility that I would be late. Although if anyone had a legitimate excuse for being late this situation would be one. However, I did not like any excuses for being late and I was not prepared to give one on my behalf. I bolted for my truck and headed home. When I said I was soaked from the waist down, that was true, fortunately, however, that soaking was limited to the front of my pants and shoes, so I was not getting any diesel on my truck seat. Yes, I did break the speed limit, both ways. After arriving home, I took off my shoes, socks, pants, and shirt and left them on the front porch. I went into the house, stripped down, and took a 60 second shower. I redressed and rushed back to my truck and headed back to school. I had left the bus parked by the gas tank. I jumped out of my truck, sprinted to the bus, and headed to the gym to pick up the junior varsity team. I opened the door of the bus for them to get on, two minutes before departure time! I finally breathed again.

Later that night after arriving home I looked at the clothes and shoes on the front porch. I thought, maybe I could wash them and get the smell out or take them to a dry cleaner and pay for them to try and get the smell out. Realization sat in. Nothing was going to get the smell of diesel fuel out of the clothes or my shoes. I went inside, got a garbage bag, put all the items into it, and took it to the outside garbage can. What was going to be a simple, boring, routine trip turned into something that no one could have ever made up.

SLIP, SLIDING AWAY: Whenever we had an away baseball game scheduled I would always use my lunch time to drive the bus we were going to use and load up the equipment needed for a game. I did this myself instead of delegating it because I wanted to make sure nothing was left behind. I wanted to do it slowly and methodically as to not overlook anything. The City of Sulligent owned the baseball field that we used as well as several other little league and softball fields. This was a big deal for our program. It meant the school was not responsible for the electric bill, water bill, or materials used to maintain the surfaces of the fields. It also allowed us over the years to greatly improve the field with outstanding bleachers, new dugouts, and new fencing. The city also had a full-time worker that would keep the fields mowed, restrooms cleaned, and the grounds policed. The baseball field is located in a unique position. The press box, which was located directly behind home plate was at the base of the city cemetery. On the third base side of the field located about 200 feet from the fence was a road that drove around the cemetery but not around the field. On the first base side of the field about 200 feet from the fence was private property. Outside of left field was the parking area for cars and visitors' buses. Beside the right field fence foul area was a building that housed materials for the park and a small building in which our baseball equipment was stored. Behind the right field area were a softball field and a little league field. A service road that connected to the main road drove between those two fields and up to and around the maintenance building. This road was barely wide enough for a single vehicle and was packed with gravel, but not asphalt. The road was also curved.

There is plenty of room for a bus to turn circle around the maintenance building, stop, and back up to the storage building. I would load the baseball equipment through the backdoor. This day was a beautiful day for baseball. It was early April, a few days past some heavy rains, but now not a cloud in the sky and warm temperatures.

After loading the equipment, I would now make the trip back through the path I had come on, take the bus to the other side of the baseball field where later that day the players would park their cars and load on the bus for the trip to the game. As I got to the apex of the curve and noticed that city workers were at the edge of the opening to the main road and had a front-end loader machine. I did not know what type of project they had going on, but I did suddenly start to feel the bus slide to the left. Not just the front, not just the back, but the entire left side of the bus. I was traveling at a slow rate of speed. This turned out to be a good thing. I was able to stop the bus by normal braking, but the bus was now sitting at about an 80-degree angle and about four feet from the outfield fence of the softball field. This was very scary. Much more movement would result in the bus completely flipping over causing tremendous damage to the bus and the softball field and possibly to me. I gently opened the bus door, and gently exited it. The city workers noticed what had happened and as if God had placed them there for that moment came over to where I was at. Not much explanation about what the situation was needed. One of the workers, who happened to be the city foreman asked if I wanted him to pull the bus out. I said, yes, if you can. Not only did they have a heavy-duty front-end loader, but also had some heavy-duty chain. They attached the chain to the bus and were able to pull it back on the road without any damage to anything.

Looking at the tracks caused by the bus sliding, it was evident that I did not drive off the edge. The best explanation is that the ground was so soft from the rain that that part of the road just slowly gave way. I did not have to call for help from the bus administrator, I was not late, and nothing other than some anxious moments came from the incident.

KEYS: Some things you learn in the classroom. Some things you learn from experience. I had learned a lot about driving a bus from the information given in a classroom, practice driving, and by driving a few substitute routes. Overall, I was lacking in experience. All my driving to this point would always end with me delivering the bus back to the school bus yard. However, I was now going to make my first trip as a driver to an away baseball game. It was going to be a fifty-minute one way drive. There was a junior varsity and a varsity game scheduled. One of the questions I had for the bus supervisor before my first substitute route was, where do I put the keys after I am finished. His answer was to leave them in the ignition.

Remember that my policy was that every player had to ride the bus to the game, but any player could ride home with their parents after the game. Remember that this was before everyone had a cell phone. We had won the varsity game and had played well in doing so. There were probably four players left that were going to ride the bus back to Sulligent. They helped me take the equipment from the field to the bus. All the parents had left before we reached the bus. With everyone on the bus, I put my seatbelt on and reached for the keys to start the bus. There was just one problem. There were not any keys in the ignition!

I was in shock and just stared at the ignition for a moment before informing the players on the bus what the situation was. We all started looking for the keys. We looked under the dash, under all the items in the front, and under every seat of the bus. Next, we went outside and looked thoroughly around it and then proceeded to do a second search of the bus, and then a third. No keys. I sat back down in the driver's seat and thought about my next move. The baseball field was not located on school property or close to the town. My only choice would be to start walking. Since I still had my baseball uniform on hopefully someone would be willing to help me, but the question would be how long it would be before I saw anyone. Just before I exited the bus a person associated with the local school drove back to the field. I explained the situation to him, and he said he would go back to the school and call my bus supervisor. About fifteen minutes later he returned telling me that indeed someone with a spare key would be on the way. It would take them about an hour to get there.

The players were now off the bus killing time. There was a large area of sand right in front of the bus. I am sure this sand was used on the baseball field when needed to fill in bare areas of grass and such. Two of the players had sat down in the sand and were playing in it with their hands. I was in the driver's seat feeling depressed because I felt like it was my fault that someone who was already home from work would now have to put in at least two more hours of work because of me, even though I did not have a clue what had happened to the keys.

Suddenly one of the players thrust his hand up in the air. In his hand was a set of keys! Was it the keys to the bus? We were about to find out. I put the keys in the ignition. I turned the keys. The bus started!

We headed back toward Sulligent. I still felt bad because I did not have any way to contact the person bringing me the spare key. He would drive all that way, see that we were gone, and then drive back home. I am sure he would not be happy about that.

One of our players had a younger brother about eight years old. A friend of his and him had discovered the sand pile while the games were being played. For some reason he decided that he needed the keys to the bus to play with in the sand. While his playing with them in the sand he lost the keys. He was too afraid to tell his parents before they left and did not own up to what had happened until they confronted him with how the keys were found.

I never left the keys in the ignition of a bus to any away baseball game ever again.

MIXING OPPOSITES: I had one of the most supportive fathers any son could ever have. In all my high school and college football careers he only missed one game and that was in college when I was dressed out but knew I would probably not play because of a slight injury. He was supportive during my coaching career also, going to as many games as possible, even when I lived far away from him. However, after he retired, and I was the baseball coach at Sulligent he never missed a home game and made the most of the away games. There were some trips we made during the playoffs that required leaving the day before the contest and spending the night. He made the most of those trips. He was on the trip during this incident.

I never liked the Alabama High School Athletic Association's playoff policy concerning high school baseball. For years, the AHSAA baseball playoff format had five rounds to it. The first three rounds were single elimination with the semi-finals and finals being a best out of two. The way that the first three rounds were played, a Saturday, the following Wednesday, then the following Saturday, it was possible that a team could pitch their best pitcher all three games and that is what would happen in the smaller classification when teams would only have one ace pitcher. We had at least three teams in my first five years at Sulligent that had a better overall pitching staff than some teams that eliminated us from the playoffs in either the first or second round. The AHSAA now has a policy in which every round of the playoffs is a best two out of three set up. The year this incident took place the AHSAA had made a change and now the quarter finals would be a best two out of three match-up with only the first and second rounds being single elimination.

We had one great pitcher, Lyle Northington, a left-hander, who would go on and pitch for UAB after high school. After him we had three above average pitchers and one who on some days could be very good. Since we had won our division during the regular season, we would be hosting the first-round game at home. Our opponent would be a team that had finished second in their division. After getting a scouting report on the team we would be playing, I decided to start a pitcher other than Northington. I felt like we could beat them without Northington pitching and that would allow us to use Northington in the second round and hopefully propel us to the quarterfinals and best two out of three match-up.

I had a sophomore who was very talented, both as a pitcher and a hitter. He was also a very big discipline problem in the classroom. I had already disciplined him by running him and sitting out a game. I had warned him that he was pushing his luck and that his conduct during school hours must improve. He had not been a discipline issue at practice or during games. He was a competitor and loved playing the game. He had so much potential. We did win the first game and now had to travel to play the second game. However, the second game would be played on the opposite side of the state about 180 miles from Sulligent. Our plan was to leave on Friday, drive to the town we would be playing in and spend the night. The game was scheduled for 1 p.m. on Saturday. Since we had just played the first-round game on Wednesday, Thursday was just going to be a light practice in terms of length of time and the type of workout we would have. Before practice I had gotten word that the player with the discipline issues had been in trouble again with a teacher. Before practice I had a talk with him. One in which he was not very receptive to what I was saying. This attitude carried over into practice to the point that I told him to leave practice and to leave the baseball facility.

The season before we were loaded with talent. Three pitchers, Eric Hollis, Justin Maddox, and of course, Northington, who would all go on and pitch on the collegiate level. However, we were eliminated in the first round in a game full of controversy. I had also lost two other seniors, besides Hollis and Maddox, that contributed greatly to the team. The team this season played the toughest scheduled we had and would play during my time at Sulligent. Even though we had won the division we did not get about the .500 level until after we had won the first playoff game. This team was close and was very excited about the upcoming trip. Most did not think a whole lot about me sending the player home during practice. I ran a tight ship, and we had rules that everyone had to follow, but I am sure none were prepared for what was going to happen.

We were going to leave at 10 a.m. The first thing I did upon arriving at school that morning was to get the bus I was going to use, load up the gear, and park it in front of the school instead of by the baseball field. I then went in and talked to my principal, told him what was about to happen, and asked him to be a witness. The principal was a strong backer of teachers. However, if a teacher was in the wrong, he would make them make it right. I called the player with the discipline issues out of class. I discussed with him some of the issues that he had been having, the times that I went the extra mile with him, but that he had finally crossed over the proverbial line in the sand at practice the day before and that I was dismissing him from the team. I made him go get his uniform, told him he would be welcome to rejoin the team next season, but he was finished for this year.

After everyone had boarded the bus, I explained what had just happened and the reasons for it. Most of the players knew of his issues but still did not expect the dismissal. They were not really upset, and most had a feeling of relief. We headed out to play in the second-round game of the playoffs and one of our best players was not coming.

In my second year at Sulligent, we had to travel to Montgomery to play our first-round playoff game. I learned that there were not many Shell gas stations that carried diesel fuel in between Sulligent and Montgomery. The reason that it had to be Shell was that is the company that our administration used for a gas credit card. We found a station on the way back from Montgomery but with only about an eighth tank of fuel remaining. I told my father that his job was to be on the lookout for Shell stations that had diesel fuel. We had plenty of fuel to get where we were going, so there was no need to fuel up until after the game on Saturday.

Northington was pitching one of his best games of the season and we were in complete control going into the bottom of the seventh inning. We had a 9-3 lead and the first two batters had struck out to start the inning. Then a routine ground ball to the shortstop. Fielded cleanly, skip, and a throw. Wide right. Error and a runner on first base. Three errors and three hits later we finally got the final out with the tying run on second base. A 9-3 lead turned out to be a 9-8 final, but I did not care as I tried to impress on the team, which felt like I was going to jump all over them, that a win is a win and we were headed to the next round, a two out of three round.

A little extra time than normal was spent with players and parents discussing that game and where the next game would possibly be played. We did know ahead of time that it would be another road contest. However, we would have to wait until the result of another game as to which school it would be at. Finally, we loaded up. My assistant coach, my father, and five players were on the bus. I reminded my father about looking for fuel and we proceeded back toward Sulligent. There was still close to half a tank of fuel in the bus. I wanted to find more fuel as soon as possible so that I could put that worry behind me. We had driven about twenty miles when I spotted a Shell station. It was on the left side of the road, and I had seen it too late to make an immediate turn, so I went a little further and went back to it.

I was still excited about the game and the future. I needed to call the result of the contest into the AHSAA and the Tuscaloosa News. I pulled up to the pumps. I picked the pump with the black handle on it, stuck it into the opening of the gas tank and started fueling. While fueling I went inside and made my phone calls. I came back to the pump just before it finished pumping. I went back in and paid for the fuel. Everything was going so smoothly. A win, reporting requirements taken care of, a full tank, now just to enjoy the ride back home.

My father sat right behind me on these trips, We usually kept a conversation going. Most of the time it was about sports. All five of the players were in the back three rows of the bus and were enjoying themselves. Suddenly, BOOM! A sound so loud that one player jumped over one seat forward into another seat. I tensed up not knowing what had happened. Everyone started laughing after the shock wore off, but it was soon not to be a laughing matter. About five miles further down the road a second loud boom sounded off. I was now concerned. My father leaned toward me and said, "son, did you put gas in the tank"? Fear gripped me. I pulled the receipt out and handed it to him and yes, I had put gas into a bus that required diesel. My father said that I had better pull over the first chance I got. That was about a mile later at what had at one time been a dinner. Of course, it was closed now. Again, before cell phones. I was sick to my stomach. I became even sicker when my father proceeded to tell me what could happen to a diesel engine if gasoline is put into it. Not only would the bus not run, but there was also a real possibility that the diesel engine would be destroyed. We had made to go to a county that was a more prosperous county than a lot in Alabama. That would be important later. I knew we needed to communicate with my administration but how? As we looked toward the old building, we noticed that there was a pay phone outside of it. Surely it was not working. I sent a player over to check it out and it turned out to be working. I was able to get in contact with my bus supervisor. He was an outstanding man. He was very calm about the situation and told me what was going to happen. He said he would call the bus supervisor for that county and that he would get them to send out a crew to see if they could fix it.

About forty-five minutes later a group of five men showed up in two trucks. Telling them of the situation, they said there was one shot in getting it to work. First, they would have to drain all the fuel out of the bus. Over 50 gallons. They would then have to replace the fuel filter with a new one. Then add enough diesel to the bus to get us to another station to fuel up. Simple enough? Of course not. The draining of the tank would require them to use five-gallon cans to put the fuel in, take those five gallons and put them in a barrel on one of the trucks so that the fuel could be properly disposed of. This would take some time as they did not want to have a lot of spillages when draining the tank. Time seemed to stand still during this process. This had now turned into a Saturday night event, and I was just wondering how much these men were hating to have to do this. However, they were very friendly and were probably enjoying the story of such a dumb ass thing that had happened. I found out that it is an unwritten policy with most counties in Alabama that if a bus breaks down from a different county that the county that the bus breaks down in will take care of the issue instead of forcing the other county to drive out and take care of their own bus. Southern hospitality.

The fuel had been drained. A new fuel filter had been put on. About 15 gallons of diesel fuel had been put in the tank. Now it was time to cross my fingers and turn the keys. I am not sure if the guys were messing with me, but they said I had one chance for it to start. Just what I needed, more pressure. The turn of the key and a powerful roar of the engine. Relief went through my entire body. I was fortunate that the bus had almost half of a tank of diesel in it before I added gasoline. That weakened the effect of the gasoline on the engine. We drove about five miles and found a Shell station that sold diesel fuel. After stopping outside the pump that had diesel fuel written across it, I made all five players get out of the bus and verify that indeed it was diesel.

SUMMARY: I take full responsibility for the diesel/gasoline incident. I was not focused on one thing at a time, and it almost turned out to be a disaster. For the others, well, read them and make up your own mind.

Chapter 6

Drills

At age 62 I did the nine-week ***INSANITY*** *workout program. I took two weeks off and did it again. Working out my entire life has helped me maintain my overall good health.*

Monkey Rolls

This was one of the most hated, but actually one of the most productive drills we did in high school. It was hated because of the physicality of it, but, looking back, it improved me as a defensive football player, probably as much as any single drill.

To begin the drill, 3 players would line up side by side on their knees and hands. They would be about two feet between each player. The drill would begin with the player in the middle rolling to his right. The player to his right would jump over him, in as much a horizontal fashion manner as possible, while rotating his body. If successful, the jumping player would land on his shoulder and roll to his left and immediately be able to jump back toward his right. At the same time the player that had originally jumped the middle player, the player to the opposite of the middle player was getting ready to jump over the first outside player who had jumped over the middle player.

Now after the middle player had started the drill by rolling to his right, as soon as he had made his roll he was up, ready to jump back toward his left. He would be jumping over the players that had originally lined up to his left.

As you can visualize, this could be a never-ending process if done correctly. In football a player is going to get knocked down. That shouldn't mean that he is done for that play. I'm sure all of you have seen plays in which a player that was originally knocked down, got back up and made the tackle on the runner, or got back up and made another block on a defensive player. In this drill, a player had to move quick, had to get out of the way of another player, and had to be more focused during the drill correctly than the pain and the better you executed the drill, the better carry over during a game.

This was a thing of beauty to watch when done correctly. And when it was done correctly the coach would only make the group do about 4-5 rolls and end the drill.

However….lol. However, correctly done was not always the case. As you can imagine, especially at the high school level, and especially at a high school with a small number of players, not all the players were of equal ability. This ability, which in this drill involved a lot of coordination and quickness, was of an even greater distance apart among linemen.

Often, larger, slower, less coordinated linemen would do one of the following. Not roll after hitting the ground, not get up fast enough after rolling, not jump high enough when trying to pass over a teammate or roll more than once after hitting the ground. As a result, several things would happen. One, of course, would be that the drill would not be executed correctly. Another would be that often a teammate would be a victim of a larger lineman falling on him during a roll. However, as you can guess the worse thing would be the wrath of the coach coming down on the players involved in the drill. This could result in anything from continuing to do the drill over and over, to a verbal lashing, to having to run sprints.

As a player, if you could execute this drill, you would be looking for two other teammates that could also do it, and they in turn would be looking for you.

So, you have pictured how the "Monkey Rolls" drill works. Nice and clean or utter chaos. Either way let me explain how the drill really turned into a monster. On some days. The coach would feel a need to add fuel to the fire in this drill. He would do this by making the players recover a "fumble". Pretty simple step to the drill, but one that added intense physical and mental tests. The coach would be in front of the players with a football. After a certain number of rolls (it might be one, it might be five) he would toss the football on the ground and it was your job to recover it. However, recovering it was not enough. You had to maintain possession of it while your two teammates tried to take it away from you, using almost whatever means necessary to achieve that task. Now, the players did not know if the coach would drop the ball in front of them, to the right, to the left, or even throw it behind them. They knew that they needed to get the "fumble". Because recovering the "fumble" usually meant that you did NOT have to do extra sit-ups or push-ups for NOT recovering the fumble.

When the 'fumble" aspect was used in the drill it made players focus on the coach with the football more than just doing the drill. The drill became second nature because now success depended on recovering the football more than just doing the drill. However, if you didn't do the drill correctly your chances of recovering the football would diminish as the coach would often "fumble" the football if one of the players messed up. This meant that the player that had done something incorrectly during the drill would probably not recover the fumble meaning he would have to do sit-ups or push-ups.

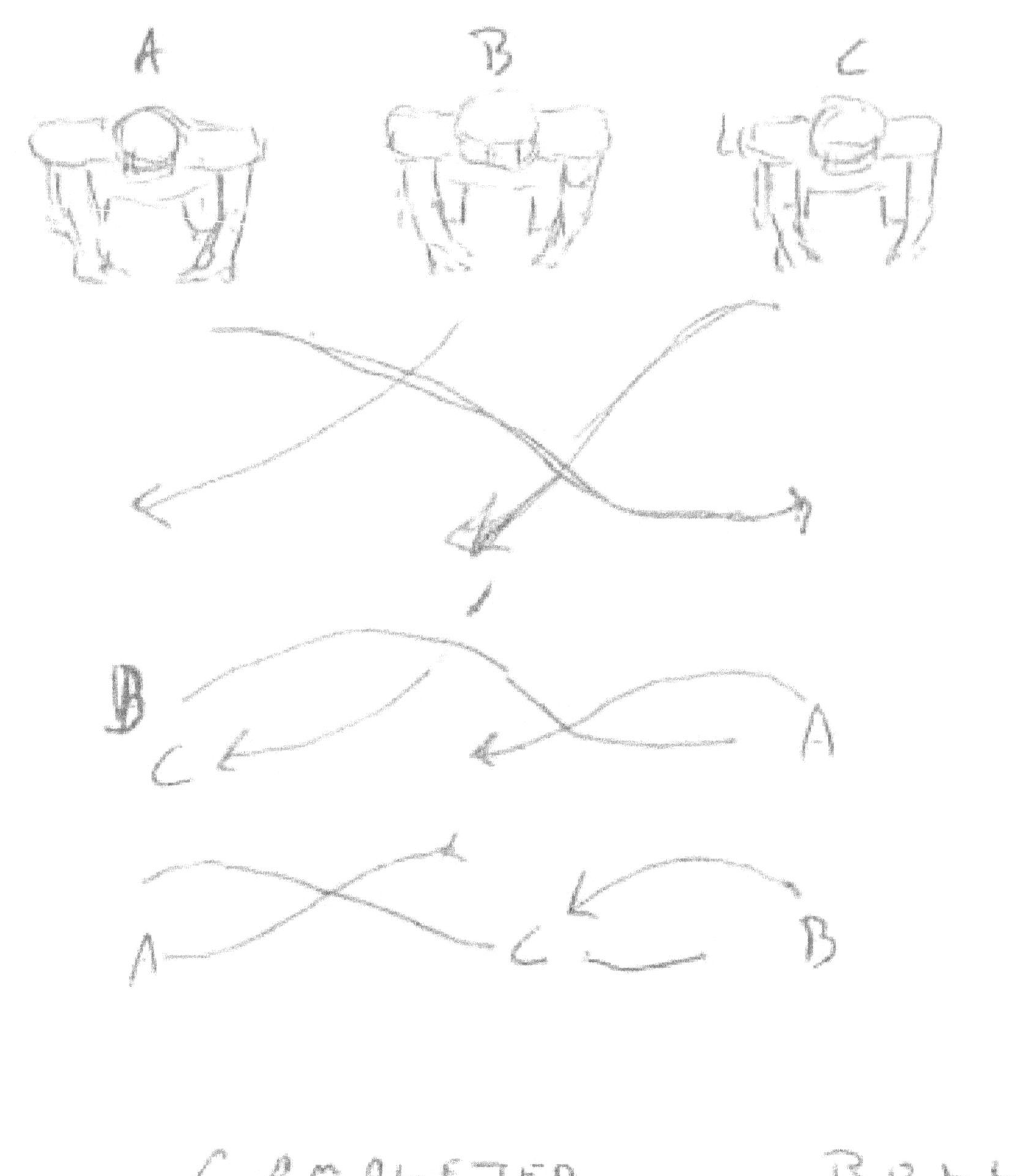

A COMPLETED ROLL

Neck Strengthening

Several drills were used to warm up the body prior to practice or a game. Most were the usual body in motion type of drills that promoted blood and oxygen flow throughout the body.

One was completely different. I never heard it being used anywhere else besides my high school. I am sure it was, but I never heard any of my teammates in college talk about doing it or any of the coaches I came across during my coaching career.

The purpose was to strengthen the neck and also get it ready for contact. A player would lie on his back, grab his facemask with both hands and wait on the command from the coach. "UP" would signal the player to push back, walk his feet up under him. While driving his head into the ground so that he would be on the crown of his helmet. He would be in a half-moon posture.

This was only the first part of the drill. After achieving this position the player would know to "work" the neck some with slight movements while maintaining this position. Now comes the fun part. A coach would say "ready". A player would become still, focus his mind, tense his body. "FLIP", would be the next command. The player would quickly, with a great kick with the right leg and a slight movement of the left while maintaining his helmet in the spot it was located, flip hiss entire body so that now he was still in a half-moon position, but his stomach was facing the ground instead of toward the sky. No part of the body, except the feet and head, should ever touch the ground in this drill after it started.

However, after achieving this flip, the drill was NOT over. The player would instinctively be ready for the next "FLIP" command. You would then flip back to the original position. Most of the time 5-6 flips would be the amount of this drill.

Quickness was emphasized in this drill, as in all drills, as it wasn't just good enough to properly execute the drill, you had to do it fast.

I like this drill and the challenge it presented. I'm not sure if it actually had any benefits for the neck, but it did make you think you were getting tougher.

Zero

Probably the most puzzling drill that I ever participated in didn't even have a name so I'm calling Zero and you will be able to figure out why. I never used it while coaching. My high school coaches used it only with linemen. It was part fun and part hell. The fun part was, as a lineman, one would catch a pass. The hell part was the one catching the pass was going to be hit squarely in the middle of the back as soon as the pass was caught.

Players would form two lines opposing one another. Line A would be the receivers, while line B would be the hitters. ON command, the player from line A would sprint about 5 yards turn back toward the coach to receive the pass. As the coach let go of the ball a player from line B would sprint toward the player catching the ball and would usually contact the other player just about the time the ball got there. Contact would be made in the middle of the back.

The key point to tis drill was if you were to catch the ball before you got hit, you were not allowed to make any type of move that would prevent the oncoming hit. If the hitter was a little bit late, well, just stand and wait on it.

I guess this was a drill developed long before my time as a means of making a player more mentally tough. It would almost be impossible for a lineman to ever hit a receiver in the back just after catching a pass, so it did not serve as any skill improvement. Linemen, of course, are ineligible, in most situations to catch a ball.so that was not going to happen in a game.

Physical and mental toughness are part of football. In this drill the coaches were doing something that promoted both, with a little fear, and the ability to overcome that fear. Fortunately, this drill was not used too often, and no one ever got hurt as a result.

Footnote: Linemen are linemen for several reasons. One is that they often are not very good at catching a pass and this would usually be the case in this drill. Of course, after the drill, all the linemen would be giving each other some good natured ribbing to those who dropped any passes and those that caught the passes would be jokingly asking the coaches for a chance at a receiver's position.

Goal Line Stand

The 1971 National Championship season would have only one blimp on it. A 21-20 loss to Troy State. Troy had converted two 4th and goal situations from the one-yard line for touchdowns. The Trojan running back had literally leaped higher than the offensive and defensive linemen, and linebackers to score. The next week a new drill was introduced at practice I like to call it "the goal line stand".

This drill was for linebackers only. There would be three players on their hands and knees. Another player would be the running back who would leap over those players on the ground. One linebacker would be in a striking position just in front of the players on the ground. When the player with the ball would leap the technique for the linebacker was to hit the ball carrier in the chest, wrap him up, and drive him backwards. He could not let him fall to the left or right because he might score. Since there was not any blocking going on this was a "kill shot" on the running back because he was leaping in a defenseless position.

The top four linebackers on the team that year were great players. Two would be All Americans and one of those would eventually be drafted by the Dallas Cowboys. It was a tough drill, especially for the ball carrier.

Bull in the Ring

Five players would circle another player, the "bull". The drill would begin with the bull running in place and circling in the one spot. He would be in a football position ready to both defend himself and deliver a blow. The players surrounding him would each have a number. After a few seconds the coach would call out a number. The player would then attack the bull and hit him regardless of if the bull was facing him or not. The purpose of the drill was to make the bull quicker, to improve his porifera vision, and be able to defend himself at the last second.

It was a very physical drill, but sometimes the bull would be in a position that he would get hit in the back by almost everyone that the coached called out. This would not be intentional by the coach, it would just be that the bull would often move from facing the player whose number was called, to away from him at the last second.

To improve the drill one adjustment was made. The bull would now point toward the player he wanted to challenge. He still had to keep moving in a stationary circle, but he could improve his technique by always meeting a player face to face. He could not point out only players that might be smaller than him or the coach would go back to the number's method of the drill.

Four Corner Wrestling

Intensity, physicality, endurance, mental toughness. These were all areas that the drill, "four corner wrestling" was meant to improve. This was an off-season drill which was very challenging, but also fun (once you had completed your turn).

Off season workouts would consist of two days a week in the weight room and two days a week in the gym. If the offensive players were in the weight room than the defensive players would be in the gym and vice versa. Every day in the gym was mentally and physically challenging. The intensity level would be as high as any point of a season, even more so than a game. On days that there was not four corner wrestling, players would go through movement drills that would be nonstop until the complete session was over.

An official size wrestling mat was used. The players would divide equally to the four corners. The coach then would determine which corner would go first. Whichever player that was in the front of that line would then enter to the center of the mat. Going in a clockwise manner, the first player in the next line would now enter on to the mat. The original player would get a hold on the second player who was in in an "all fours" position. When the coach would blow his whistle, wrestling would begin. This "wrestling" was not like any you had seen before. There were not any "moves" or pinning anyone. It was just short of a fight with constant motion. If one player had another pinned, he would have to let him go and the wrestling would continue. If a player could drive another into the mat, pick him up and drive again that was encouraged.

The original player would wrestle that first player for 20 seconds, the second player would exit and then player one from the next line would enter and the original player would wrestle him for 20 seconds. The original player's turn would be over after he wrestled the first player from the last corner.

The original player would go to the end of his line and recover for a few seconds before he was expected to be back to encourage his group. Everyone in the original line would follow this same pattern. After everyone had went in the original line then the process started with the next line. This meant that every player would wrestle two minutes. One complete minute as the wrestler and 3 twenty-minute sessions as a challenger.

Two minutes? Doesn't sound like much. Almost everyone would be beat on that last 20 second match. Going nonstop for 40 seconds before entering that last match, with a fresh player, would almost always mean that you were not going to win the last session. But you had better not lay down unless you wanted to go through the complete session again. There would be at least four coaches with the drill, all "encouraging" you and all your other teammates "vocalizing" their comments during the sessions. Players in each corner would match themselves with other players from the other corners to the same ability as theirs.

The drill accomplished it's intended goal and it also helped players create a bond with each other.

Just to understand the drill a little bit better, go outside and sprint wide open for 40 seconds., Stop for 2 seconds, and then sprint wide open for another 20 seconds. And that would be without any of the physical contact, Enjoy.

Bounce Up

Two players, in full pads, would be laying on the ground, on their backs, with the tops of their helmets touching, and bodies pointing in opposite directions. On the coaches' whistle they would get up as fast as possible and then attack the other players. One of the goals would be to attack the other player in a good defensive technique and take him to the ground. The faster you got up the better your chances were that you could deliver the blow instead of absorbing it. However, if both players got up at the same time, even if proper technique was not used, one player had to take the other to the ground before the drill would end. You had a few seconds of concentration before the coach blew his whistle to start the drill.

Football requires concentration, intensity, physicality, and sudden movements, and this drill contained all of those.

Chapter 7

Leadership

Sometimes you do not have to look very far for leaders

Leadership and Leaders

Everyone is affected by the leaders that are in their life. Sometimes these leaders are negative in their leadership, but hopefully most will be positive. One of the main reasons for the success I have had in my life is that, for the most part, I have been surrounded by great leaders with a positive outlook on life and the professions they were in.

LEADERSHIP: Leadership is the ability of an individual or a group of individuals to influence and guide followers or other member of an organization.

The Characteristics & Qualities of a Good Leader.

- Integrity
- Ability to delegate
- Communication
- Self-awareness
- Gratitude
- Learning Agility
- Influence
- Empathy
- Courage
- Respect

The following is a list of people who played positive roles in my life either by their leadership, the way they conducted themselves, or doing things that would seem to have been above their capabilities.

The two greatest leaders in my life were Dabbs Earnest and Jim King.

Dabbs Earnest: Coach Earnest came to Sulligent in the fall of 1968. He was such a humble man that most of the students, and even the players he coached, did not know his background until after he had been on the job for a couple of years. However, his humbleness did not get in the way of his stern, but fair leadership, his physical demands of a player, his expectations that a player would be coachable, and that his players would never embarrass the program by negative vocal or physical actions toward him, other players on the team, opponents, officials, or fans. He was very serious about his coaching, and he expected the same outlook from his players. He was intimidating, but not overbearing. He cared about his players more than he did winning and he expected his players to be first class citizens, not only on the court or field, but also in the classroom and in the community. He was an All American at Florence State University in Florence, Alabama, as both a basketball and baseball player. He brought this success in both sports to Sulligent, where he won 100 games in 5 seasons as head basketball coach and went 32-13 in his three seasons as baseball coach, winning two division titles and finishing state 2A runner-up in his third year. He carried himself in a way that did not bring attention to himself but exuded confidence. His players, the ones that stuck with him, loved him. He did not have favorites and put the team above everything else, Including himself.

Jim King: Coach King was the offensive line coach when I went to Livingston University in the falloff 1971. Since I was a defensive player, our paths did not cross much in 1971, and since I did not play in 1972, I did not really know him. What I did know about him came from me being on the scout team defense going against the first team offense. He was very intense and wanted perfection from his offensive linemen. The offensive line must work in tandem more than any other group on a football team. They must make decisions at the line of scrimmage after the play has been called, often against defenses that will change alignment from play to play and even change alignment once the offense has come to the line of scrimmage. They must be some of the more mentally aware players on the team and they must set the tone for physicality for the offense. Coach king embodied all these features. He was an outstanding offensive lineman at the University of Southern Miss, being named team captain.

After the 1972 season, Coach Mickey Andrews left Livingston to become the head coach at Florence State University. Coach King was hired as his replacement. Coach King was wise enough to know that he did not have to make a lot of changes, but to add his touch to the program, build on the previous success, and keep the Tigers as a dominant force in the GSC.

Coach king not only assumed the responsibilities of head coach, but he left the offensive line to become defensive coordinator. In January of 1973, he gave me a chance to come back to Livingston. He did not make any extra stipulations on my return and treated me like I had never left. That was a sign of a true leader. Since he was now the defensive coordinator, I got to know him better real fast. He was as intense as Coach Andrews but would also bring some humor to the field at the appropriate time. We ran the same defense that had been successful for the Tigers in the past the first two seasons that Coach King was defensive coordinator but switched to a little different scheme in his third year. He also coached a position group but was active with every position. He encouraged players to do their best and the players responded to his personality which was one of being intimidating with expectations, but father-like at the same time. He developed the wisdom of pushing a player to his limit, but no beyond it. He demanded a player put the team first, to be on time for meetings and practice, and to represent the team off the field in a first-class manner. We did not have many issues as a team under his watch.

Coach King's wisdom also came into play during the cultural change of the 70's. When players went to him about some of the traditions that had been in place, not only at Livingston, but most colleges, particularly the shaving of heads he listened. He would not always give the players what they wanted but he did end that tradition. It was not by any big announcement, but he also let players to grow breads and moustaches and to allow their hair to be long. He did not really like it, but he knew it was important to the players. Coach King knew how to handle a loss. He usually did not have an immediate response after a game but would wait until after he had seen the game film. He was not hesitant to take any blame that he deserved for a loss and seldom used the words "I" of "me" in responding to a win or any success we had. Coach King was steady and predictable. Players knew what he expected every day and responded to that type of leadership.

Assets: I know I will leave someone off this list that played important roles in who I became, and I apologize for that. However, I feel the need to list the following.

- Mickey Andrews: Coach Andrews had played for Bear Bryant at Alabama and brought the intensity that Bryant displayed to Livingston. He was the most intense coach I have ever known during a game.
- Lemuel Boyett: Lemuel was the purest shooter I have ever seen in basketball. He had perfect form and was almost indefensible with his turnaround jump shot. He holds the single game record for Sulligent with 52 points and lettered four years at Livingston.
- Freddie Carruth: Three years older than me Freddie was a great athlete and excelled at football and basketball. As a senior he took me under his wing when I was a 9th grader, encouraging me instead of harassing me as sometime the case is when that much age difference is in play. He had SEC talent as a wide receiver but struggled in the classroom.
- Danny Cox: Danny was a defensive back at Livingston. He did not have a lot of playing time over his career, but he was an inspiration because he was missing one hand. He brought determination to the practice field every day and made me appreciate what I had been blessed with.

- Jack Crowe: Coach Crowe was just a few years older than the players at Livingston, but his personality separated us immensely in a positive way. He was very intelligent and demanded perfection. Perfection was also something he demanded from himself.
- Paul Davis: Paul was a senior with me in 1975. He was an undersized inside linebacker but played with intensity and was known for his playing his technique to almost perfection and his ability to escape blocks.
- Tony Davis. Tony came to Sulligent as a guidance counselor when I was in the eighth grade. I would wind up working for him over 30 years later when he was principal of Sulligent High School. I learned a lot about how to deal with parents by watching him.
- C. D. Elliott: Coach Elliott was my high school football coach for four years. He brought toughness to the program and guided us to the 2A state playoff semifinals in 1971.
- Jeff Finch: Jeff was athletic director at Nettleton (MS) high school when I was hired there. Not only was I moving from one school to another, but I was moving from one state to another. He treated me like a brother and helped me tremendously while I was coaching baseball.
- Carlos Flynn: One of my best friends. He was small, but excelled in football, basketball, and baseball. His best sport was as the shortstop on our baseball team. He threw right-handed but batted left-handed. As the leadoff hitter for our team, he always had a high batting average.
- Jimmy Graham: My first coach in any sport. He was my little league coach. He was also a coach of the high school teams.
- Kenneth Hand: Kenneth was a versatile player who could have played offense if needed but played most of his career as a defensive back for Livingston. Kenneth was a good player, but he also helped team chemistry with his outgoing personality.
- Danny Hollis: Danny was a tremendous backer of the baseball program at Sulligent while I was there. He was able to secure funds to improve the baseball facility over the years, but not just any funds, he wanted everything to be first class and would not settle for anything less. Although, he was the father to the most successful player I ever coached he never once asked for special favors.
- Gary Holmes: Even smaller than Paul Davis, Gary excelled at inside linebacker particularly as a senior on the 1975 team when he was named to the GSC first team defense. Very tough.

- Tony Holmes: One of the best offensive linemen ever at Livingston. Was an All American by also probably the main leader of the offense in 1975. His blocking technique was next to perfect and was a determined, dedicated player.
- Kenneth Humbers: Was in my senior class. He was the Most Valuable Offensive player for the Blue Devils for three straight years. He was named as the Birmingham News 2A offensive player of the year in 1970. At 5'10 and weighing 220 pounds he was a bruising runner with speed. Instead of running out of bounds he would often turn back into the field and attack a defensive player. He was also the best player on our baseball team as a pitcher and hitter.
- Roger Humbers: Nicknamed "Stump" because of his 5'8 180-pound frame, he was as tough as a pine knot in a stump. He played middle linebacker and guard for the Blue Devils. He got everything out of his ability.
- Ken Hutcherson: Ken was one of the greatest players ever at Livingston. He was an All American who was drafted and played for the Dallas Cowboys. Ken was a devout Christian but was also one of the first Black players to attend Livingston. He had a great personality and those around him, loved him.
- Joe Allen Jaggers: He was in my senior class and helped me become a better player. He stood 6'5 and weighed 300 pounds. This is huge for any time, but especially for 1970. He played nose guard and dominated centers but was often doubled teamed. Since Joe did not play offense, I had to practice against him every day. There was no such thing as a day off practicing against him and I give him credit for making me a better center.
- David Johnson: Another outstanding offensive lineman for the Tigers. We were close friends who helped each other get by the grueling demands of college football.
- Randolph Johnson: One of the first Black players at Sulligent. He was certainly the first great player at Sulligent in football and Basketball. Randy was a humble man who would help anyone he could. He would have probably been one of the first Blacks to be signed to play SEC football if it had not been for a knee injury late in the season.
- Stanley King: Stanley transferred to Livingston in 1975. He was a great addition to our defense. He had 10 interceptions and was named GSC Defensive Player of the Year. Also known for his vicious hitting ability Stanley would be a three time All American as a Tiger.
- Mike Knight: Mike was a close friend who moved to Sulligent from Milwaukee while in junior high. It was a move that would greatly benefit Sulligent. Mike was an intense competitor

who also put that intensity into his class work. Mike was an outstanding receiver in football, guard in basketball, and in baseball as a second baseman who had "clean" hands and a good hitter. Mike would walk on at Florence State University, win a scholarship, and start several games for the Lions before a severe finger injury would end his career. He was named to the Nicholls State Athletic Hall of Fame as their winningest baseball coach in their history.

- Sam McCorkle: Sam was the center for the 1971 national championship team. He was probably the most intense player that I have ever been around. He also carried that intensity to his long coaching career in both high school and college. Undersized for an offensive lineman, Sam was a greet blocker who possessed quickness and great technique. He was named to the Livingston team of the Decade for the 1970's.
- Mike Morrison: Mike was an undersized offensive lineman but was like glue when it came to blocking a defender. He might not "pancake" an opponent, but if his opponent made a tackle Mike was still blocking him. Mike always had a smile on his face even in the hardest of practices or games.
- Mike Mixon: The quarterback of our 1970 playoff team, Mike was the one that kept everyone loose. He was a good quarterback, but his best talent came as the point guard on our basketball team. Mike loved Pete Maravich and emulated his style on the court. Mike was a great friend.
- Wayne Pitts: Wayne is my cousin who is four years older than me. He was someone I looked up to. His focus was on football, and he was a great running back. After his sophomore season there was a coaching change at Sulligent and Wayne moved to Columbus, Ms. He started for Columbus as a junior and senior and signed a football scholarship with Ole Miss. As a seventh grader during Wayne's junior year, I witnessed an inspirational play by him that would stick with me through my playing days. Wayne would sometimes play linebacker for Columbus and on one play he got his helmet knocked off during the play. Instead of picking it up he continued to chase the opponent, eventually assisting on the tackle. That was toughness.
- Jimmy Ray: Another close friend Jimmy was an undersized but intense competitor. He got the most out of his ability and never turned away from a challenge by the usually larger opponents. He was a starter in the secondary on the football team, starter a first baseman/pitcher on the baseball team and contributed to the basketball team.

- Harry Rawlinson: A close friend at Livingston who was a quiet but powerful fullback for the Tigers. He contributed greatly to the 1975 team's success.
- Russell Reeves: Russell was a senior on Sulligent's 1966 2A State championship team. He was a huge offensive and defensive lineman with a powerful playing technique. He was also very intelligent as he would eventually become a brain surgeon. I was in the eighth grade but was practicing with the varsity. I still vividly remember the practice when he got onto me for not doing my "jumping-jacks" properly. He did not do it to embarrass me, but, as a leader, he wanted everyone to be the best they could be for the team even if you were an eight-grader.
- Frank Rudowski: A senior on the 1975 Livingston team, Frank was a two-year starter for the Tigers who would be named All American that year. Frank was not big for a defensive lineman, but he played almost perfect technique. Along with his playing style, his toughness made him almost impossible to block one-on-one.
- Ricky Seale. Ricky was a close friend who was one of the quarterbacks on the 1975 team. As a sophomore he split playing time at the quarterback position which required much discipline and toughness in running the wishbone offense. Probably his most famous game came against Southeastern Louisiana when he scored four touchdowns. The game proceeded that morning, that while taking a bath, his wife accidently knocked a blow dryer that was on into the bath water. Luckily Ricky got out in time before any damage occurred.
- Clemit Spruiell: I do not believe leaders are born. I believe they are made. However, if anyone was born a leader it was Clemit. I had the good fortune to experience Clemit's leadership at two important times of my career. Once as an eighth grader when, as a senior, he led the Blue Devils to the state championship and again., as a freshman, when I watched him lead the Tigers to the National Championship. Clemit was always under control. He did not let any chaos around him distract him from his job. He came with a business-like attitude toward practice and games, but you could also see and feel the intensity in his voice and actions. Clemit was inspirational in my return to Livingston, and I will always be grateful.
- Larry Yancy: Larry was my first varsity coach. He was the head coach of the 1966 state champions Blue Devils. Coach Yancy was even going but was focused and organized. As the team was so good that year, he did not hesitate to put me in when we had a big lead. I would play some in every game but one that year. Coach Yancey made a statement at the football banquet that year that would both challenge me and inspire me. When handing me my certificate he said, "look out

for this one in the future. He is going to be good". Of course, I turned beet red and returned to my seat as fast as possible, but it gave me a reason to work harder to help his words come true.

Dabbs Earnest

A leader of men, but a "father" to boys. Look at the intensity in his face. Everyone learned how to be a positive role model from him.

Jim King

Intense, dedicated, a winner, and a demander of perfection, Coach King was still a "players coach".

Above: A surprise guest speaker at the Lamar County HOF ceremony.

Right: Pre-season publicity

LEAD TIGERS — Livingston University head football Coach Jim King is all smiles when he thinks about this pair of LU Tigers, defensive end Jerry Pitts (56) of Sulligent and fullback Ricky Austin (48) of Chatom. Both were All-Gulf South Conference choices in 1974 and should play a major role in the Bengal game plan against Tuskegee Saturday in Livingston.

Nothing but leaders on this page. Above: Seniors of 1975 and Coach King. 36-Gary Holmes, 72-Tony Holmes, 32-Kenneth Hand 55-Paul Davis, 75-Teddy Saenz, 66-David Johnson, Coach King, 62-Orville Miller, 56-myself Right: Coach King and one of the greatest to ever play for the Tigers, Ken Hutcherson

One of my most cherished awards was being named captain for the Defense. Going out for the coin toss Was always a thrill. I am the last player to the right. Our opponent for the day was Nicholls State-1975

Right: My cousin, Wayne, as a senior at Lee High School in Columbus, Mississippi, and me as An eighth grader at Sulligent. 1966

Two heroes. My son, Nathan, who swerved in the Air Force, and my father, Leon, who at age 17, served in the Navy in the Pacific arena during WWII. The above picture would be our last sporting event together as he would pass the following February.

Chapter 8

Sportsmanship

Helping the Jacksonville State University quarterback to his feet after I sacked him

Sportsmanship

Definition of Sportsmanship: **Conduct** (such as fairness, respect for one's opponent, and graciousness in winning or losing) becoming to one participating in a sport: fair play, respect for opponent, and polite behavior by someone who is competing in a sport or other competition.

One of the pillars of athletics that I was taught at a young age was to always show sportsmanship. Show it to your opponents, your teammates, to the officials, to your coaches, and to the fans. Do not being attention to yourself. Realize that if you are successful at a sport then there have been several other people involved in helping you achieve that success. Even in individual sports like golf and tennis a participant has had coaches and trainers involved.

Most of the sports we watch today does not have players that exhibit sportsmanship during a game. They are running their mouths at opponents, complaining about every call that goes against them, and often arguing with their own teammates and coaches. Announcers want to pass it off as "intensity". I call it a lack of self-discipline. How many "bat flips" do you see a baseball player do when he strikes out, which is a lot more often than when he hits home runs. How many times do you see a basketball player point at himself when the player he is guarding hits a three-pointer? How often does a defensive player get up and draw attention to himself after getting blocked like he does after a quarterback sack?

In most cases your opponent has worked as hard as you and wants to win as much as you. Do everything you can legally to beat your opponent, but do it with class, humility, and respect. Because if you don't....karma is a bitch!

Sportsmanship, we need more of it.

Chapter 9

Second Chances

Could I have been a high school running back? I never asked

Second Chance

I do not contemplate very often over the "could have been", or the "what if's" of life. What good does if do? Accept that you have been living God's plan for you and enjoy the moment. However, there are a few things that I do think about from time to time, wishing I had had a second chance with the following topics.

High School Ankle Injury: As discussed in a previous chapter I injured my ankle on the last day of practice before the 1969 season ended. This happened on a Wednesday with the last game scheduled that Friday. Even without the proper treatment I wish I had had the ankle taped, put on my shoes, and taped again. I've always wondered if I could have played with the pain, at least well enough to snap for kicks.

Poke in the Eye: The 1970 football season had been an amazing experience. It was my Senior year, and we were 9-1-1 and scheduled to play Addison in the semifinals of the 2A State Championship playoffs. It was being played at Sulligent and it was one of the biggest crowds that had ever assembled for a football game, not just at Sulligent, but for the entire area. We were slight underdogs. We kicked off to Addison. On the first play from scrimmage, I blitzed from the right side. I was untouched and had a clean shot at the running back. I arrived almost at the same time the handoff from the quarterback to the running back happened. In a reaction, the running back put his hand up toward me and a finger went into my right eye. I was stunned and had to pause for a second. Meanwhile, the running back broke for a 20-yard gain, as I gave chase. I could not see out of that eye until the second half, but I did not miss a play. Addison had more talent than we did and won the game, but I always wondered what would have happened if I had not been poked in the eye and had tackled the running back for a loss.

Missed Basket: We were playing Vernon for the Lamar County Championship. It was the 1970-71 season. My Senior year. Every game that we played against Vernon that year was close and this one was no different. Early in the fourth quarter we were down by four points. The situation was that we were inbounding the ball under our basket. The play, a pick play, was called and we executed it beautifully. I was wide open under the basket, two feet from the goal. The problem was I should have been three feet. I received the ball, shot it, hit the side of the rim. The basketball came straight back to me. I shot it again and again I hit the side of the rim. This time Vernon got the rebound. We lost the game by fie points. I should have made the basket.

Wild Pitch or Passed Ball: In the state baseball playoffs we had made the long trip to Huntsville to play Madison Academy in the quarterfinals. It was a close, back and forth game. The situation was that it was the bottom of the 7th, 2 outs, with Madison Academy having a runner on third base. We were leading by one run. On the second pitch, as our pitcher went into his delivery, I noticed the Madison Academy runner breaking full speed toward home. The base runner was about my size. The pitch was low and inside. It went by me and to the backstop. The Madison Academy runner scored easily. To this day, I do not know if it was a wild pitch or a missed ball, regardless, I should have stopped it. It would have been a giant collision at home plate, and I always wondered what the result would have been. We went on to win the game in extra innings.

Metal Bats: After the Town of Sulligent built a new baseball field, with an outfield fence, my teammates and me started hitting a few home runs. This was accomplished with wood bats. I graduated high school in 1971 and in 1976 I had my first job as an assistant football and basketball coach, and head baseball coach. During that five-year period metal bats had been developed and approved for use for high school competition. It had an immediate impact on the game. Teams were hitting home runs at record high levels and batting averages were skyrocketing. A couple of times I had taking batting practice and, even after being away from baseball as a player for over five years, was hitting 1 out of every 3 pitches over the field. I would have loved for the Sulligent Blue Devil Baseball team of 1971 to have had metal bats.

Running Back? During the summer of 1970 excitement was high in the Sulligent community for the upcoming football season. We had several experienced seniors and several talented underclassmen returning. We had good leadership and with the knowledge that the AHSAA had expanded the football playoffs from four to eight teams, we were ready to get started. I had been playing sports year-round for the last eight years. I was the catcher on the baseball team, a forward on the basketball team, and a center and linebacker on the football team. I was not just a particular player; I was an athlete. I was 6'205 pounds. I also was as fast as our starting fullback. About a week into fall practice, I had an idea that I thought would help the team. I thought about this idea for a few days and then decided to talk about it with our head coach. I was going to ask him if I could be moved to one of the halfback positions. My focus was still being a linebacker, but I felt like with my size and speed to go along with our fullback's size and speed, 5'10, 220 pounds, that we would have an almost unstoppable run game. I was not trying to usurp any of the glory from my teammate. I knew he was the best in the state. My idea was that I could be more effective blocking as a lead back for him than just blocking from the center position. I also thought that if I carried the ball about 10 times a game, he would be fresher in the fourth quarter. I just wanted to win and go to the playoffs. I went to the field house an hour earlier than normal. The head coach was already there, and I had to walk by his small office to get to my locker. The door was open, and we had a small greeting. I should have gone in immediately. At that point I had my courage up. I stayed at my locker for a few minutes and decided to try again. I headed toward his office and about the time I got there he looked up. I continued to walk. After a few minutes outside I headed back in. I did not even slow down this time as I made my way to my locker. At my locker I was telling my self how stupid it was not to just go in and talk to him. This was going to be my fourth year to play for him, we had a good relationship, and I was one of the team leaders. I arose and headed to his office. As I got there, he again looked up, surely wondering what was going on, but he did not say anything, and I kept walking. I was very disappointed in myself but resigned to the fact that I was not going to ask him to let me move to halfback. What might have been, never was because I never asked. If you have a goal do not be afraid to ask. The worse that can happen is that you get a “no”.

Weight Room: My father bought me a 125-pound barbell set from Sears when I was in the seventh grade. Using it in as many different lifts as I could I had a major growth spurt. My strength also increased rapidly. I was already stronger for my age than normal because of all the outside activity that I had done growing up in the country. I quickly got stronger than what the weight set would challenge me with. As an example, I had to do 50 repetitions with the total 125 pounds to have any effect when doing calf raises or squats. We did not have any weights, much less a weight room when I went to school at Sulligent. Today, they have a very large, first-class weight room stocked with plenty of free weights and machines. I often wonder how much stronger and larger I would have gotten in high school if we had that weight room, with a coach that knew what he was doing running it.

Defensive Coach: Our defense in high school was called a 5-3. That meant that the front of the defense would have a nose guard that lined up right in front of the center, two defensive tackles that would line up just slightly inside of the offensive tackles and two defensive ends. There would be three linebackers. One that lined up behind the nose guard and tow outside linebackers that lined up behind the defensive tackles. We had three defensive backs, a free safety who line up in the middle of the field, and two cornerbacks that lined up on the hash marks, or on any receiver that might be positioned further than the hash marks.

We did a good bit of tackling drills, but very little technique work related to each position. I was right outside linebacker. No one swapped sides regardless of the formation of the offense, where the ball was spotted or the location of the field that the ball was at. We did change a bit for our goal line defense and id the ball was on one hash the outside linebacker to the opposite, and wider side would move out a few yards.

The philosophy about defense that the head coach had was to be aggressive and run to the football. We were coached about angles a bit, but other than that everyone was going toward the ball carrier. Bing aggressive meant that at least one linebacker would be blitzing on every play. Occasionally, the offense would run a play in which we did not blitz a linebacker but that was rare. Our defensive signals were "very" complex. If the coach held up one finger that meant that the middle linebacker would blitz. If he held up two fingers that meant the left outside linebacker would stunt and if he held up three fingers that meant that the right outside linebacker would stunt. We would also do combination stunts with the coach holding up fingers 1-2, 2-3, 1-3, or even 1-2 and 3. Also to make it even simpler the linebackers would pat either the left or right buttocks of the player in front of them. This meant that they would go into either the right or left gap in front of them and the linebacker would be stunting between the opposite one. Our defensive preparation for the offense of our upcoming opponent would be for 30 minutes on the Wednesday, just before we would go over the kicking game. Most of this preparation would only show us the formations that the offense would line up in plus some of their favorite players. We would watch about 45 minutes of game film on the opponent, but other than that, "run to the ball"!

We had a great defense as far as results were concerned but knowing what I know now, how much better we could have been every year if we had had a defensive coordinator. A defensive coordinator that would take the films of opponents, look for their tendencies, who were their biggest threats, what adjustments we needed to make to counter their strengths, and what to expect in down and distance situations. A defensive coordinator that would make a player play his position, to look for reverses and counters, that somctimes it is better to wait and let the play develop than to just run to the ball.

Failed Coverage: We had started the 1975 season at Livingston by winning our first 3 games. We now knew that we could have a special season. Our fourth opponent was the Troy State

Trojans. It would be a home game. Troy had a significant win-lost advantage over Livingston, but in the previous 4 season the teams had split the games with Troy winning both of theirs by one point. It would be a huge challenge.

The previous week we had played Mississippi College, had won, and I had enjoyed what would be my single best individual game of my college career. I had 11 individual tackles, 4 assists, and 2 interceptions and was named the Gulf South Conference Defensive Player of the Week.

I was playing defensive end in 1975. However, my techniques and responsibilities were the same from the previous two season. We had switched from a 4-3 Pro style defense to a 5-2 front. It did not affect me much, but the biggest change is that we went from four defensive linemen and one linebacker inside to three defensive linemen and two inside linebackers. Troy State had a great tight end, Billy Dixon, who would also be first team All-GSC, and I would be lining up on him every play. We exploded in the first quarter with two touchdowns, one on a 91-yard run by quarterback Willie Slater on the third play of the game. However, those two touchdowns would be the end of the scoring for us. We a missed field goal that be huge later in the game.

Troy State had managed to put 10 points on the board after falling behind fourteen points and had the ball and was driving late in the game. They were converting third down situations and had pushed to our 7-yard line with less than a minute to go. They called a running play on second down which we stopped for no gain. One of the reasons we stopped them was that we had called an "FS Stunt" which meant the two safeties would blitz between the offensive guard/tackle slot, basically making an 11-man defensive front. Troy State called timeout. The "FS Stunt" was great against the run, but very weak against the pass. It was now third down. My technique on an "FS Stunt" was to cover the tight end man-to-man if a pass play developed. Troy came to the line of scrimmage in the same formation as the previous play. We had called the "FS Stunt" again. The quarterback took longer than usual calling the signals. The ball was snapped, the quarterback faked a handoff to the running back and gently floated a pass in the waiting hands of the tight end. As the ball was about halfway to the tight end I turned and started running toward him. It was too late. Dixon caught it and Troy goes ahead with 36 seconds left in the game.

I had not been disciplined enough to read my keys, stay with the tight end, and defend the pass. I was guessing that it would be another running play. The quarterback had audibled to the pass play once he seen we were about to run the "FS Stunt" again.

The Troy State game was always physical, and this was no exception. I broke my left hand in the second quarter. The trainer padded it up and I went back into the game on the next series. In the third quarter I was the target on a vicious crack back block during a sweep play that Troy was running. The blocker's forearm caught me in my neck and the first thing of mine that hit the ground was my back. I walked straight to the sideline and missed about five plays, to catch my breath and be able to talk again, before returning to the game. Those things hurt physical, but not near as bad as missing my assignment on the touchdown play.

I might not have been able to cover him, but then again, I will never know. I did not give myself a chance. It would have been easier to accept that if in the process of me covering him that he had made the catch instead of me watching him catch it uncontested.

O, for a second chance.

The Second Chance That Counted: Everything I have talked about so far are "second chances" that go through my mind with wonder about what might have been. However, I did receive a second chance that altered my life and put it on a trajectory for success that saved me from a lifetime of physical labor. I had been out of football for about 13 months. I had developed a hunger and a need to play the game again. I started looking for options but was hitting brick walls. The one option I had not tried was a return to Livingston. I did not believe that they would ever want me on their campus again. I had played the entire 1971 season but did not return to school the following January. I did not quit during the season, but I thought that the coaches would have considered me a quitter since I did not return. However, my dad, being a wise man, did consider that an option. He called the Livingston coaches without my knowledge and told them that I was looking to play college football again somewhere. The person he called was Clemit Spruiell, who had played at Sulligent and was also the quarterback of the 1971 National Championship team. Clemit talked with Coach Jim King who had recently been announced as the new head coach of the Tigers and informed him of the situation. Shortly after that, my dad tells me one evening that they are about to call me and will probably invite me back to play based on my conversation with them. When the call came Clemit was on the line with Coach King listening. He then gives the phone to Coach King and then we have a conversation. He invites me back and offers to give me a full scholarship! I drive to Livingston early the next day and begin to live my second chance. I owe my life to my dad, several times over, but particularly this time and I also owe it to Coach King. Coach Jim King was full of wisdom. He took over the Tiger football program knowing it was in good shape and that he did not have to make a lot of changes only improve what was there. He knew I could play, but he also knew that my family could not afford to send me to college and that it would take a while for me to get back into top playing form. He gave me a reason to return to Livingston and, although he was tough, he did not try to run me off or test me beyond my capabilities. He wanted to succeed, and he wanted me to succeed. We both did.

Forever thankful, Coach King, for my real second chance.

Chapter 10

Livingston Who?

Livingston *"Who"*

Livingston. The only time I had heard that name before the spring of my senior year was in the quote, "Dr. Livingston, I presume?" I did not know there was a town in Alabama named Livingston, much less that there was a Division II college, Livingston University, located there. What is now known as the University of West Alabama, the college was chartered in 1835 as a church-related female academy. The Livingston Female Academy and State Normal College continued as a private institution until 1907 when the State assumed full control. In 1929 the school became the State Teachers College. Male students were admitted but it remained predominately female through the 1950s. In 1957 the name was changed to Livingston State College and the Graduate Division was established. In 1967 the legislature created Livingston University, with its own Board of Trustees. In 1995 the institution changed its name to the University of West Alabama.

To me, because of my time spent there, it will always be Livingston University. "LU". "Give Them Hell Big L". and "Tigers". They all were used to describe the sports teams at Livingston. Our helmets had LU on the side and the official logo was a tiger climbing through an LU that had the U halfway lower than the L.

My head high school football coach, C. D. Elliott, who had played at Livingston, took me and some game film on a visit to Livingston University. I left with a full scholarship. In a few short months I would be understanding the difference between high school football and college football. Mickey Andrews, who played under Bear Bryant at Alabama, was using the exact coaching style and philosophy as Bryant's. Division II teams have some players that could play at the Division I level but most are just a little less talented and a little bit slower. However, the standards, demands, expectations, and the physical and mental challenges on the body are just as great as any Division I school.

I was a freshman member of the 1971 National Championship team. I was not on the 1972 team that went back to the playoffs, but I returned in 1973 and played for three years. During my playing time we were 35-10-1, and with the 1972 team going 8-1-2 it was one of the best, if not the best, five year stretches in their history with a combined record of 43-11-3 and with three national playoff appearances.

However, this story is not about those seasons. It would take a complete book to write about everything that took place during that era. This is about one game. The "Livingston Who?" game.

The 1975 season started off with a lot of promise. There were a lot of players returning from the previous 8-3 season plus we also had added some talented transfers. It basically was a great, but bittersweet, season until the morning after the final game when we, unexpectedly, found out that we would be going to the Division II playoffs. The sweet part had been the 9 victories. The bitter part was heartbreaking losses to Troy State, 17-14, and Jacksonville State, 17-13.

The final game of the season was a road game against UT-Martin located in Martin, Tennessee. It was played in temperatures below freezing with a howling wind the entire game. We prevailed 17-7 and my college football career had ended. At least that is what I thought. I did not ride back with the team instead went to my parents' house after the game. After spending most of the next day there I headed back to Livingston, whereas now I was just a regular student who had classes the next day. Upon pulling up to my apartment on campus another player, who seemed if he had been waiting for hours came to us, excited, wanting to know where we had been, and asking if we had heard the news. "What news?" "We are going to the playoffs!" was his answer. We did not believe him at first. He said that we had missed a team meeting about the details. We were not the only ones that had missed it, but we would be practicing the next day for the first-round game.

The first-round game was against North Dakota, the number one ranked team in the nation.

The next afternoon we had a team meeting. Coach Jim King went over several details like when we would depart for the trip, where we would be staying, practice times after we arrived, kick-off time, weather conditions, etc. He also told us that we had been selected ahead of Nicholls State who had won the Gulf South Conference. The reason that we were selected ahead of them was that we had the same amount of conference losses, but they had played one more conference game than we had which gave them a better percentage, that we had beaten them 13-7 earlier in the year, and that Livingston, at that time, had a better football reputation than they did.

After the team meeting, we broke up into offensive and defensive groups. Excitement was still in the air as we moved to another room to watch film on the Sioux. When the lights went down, and the projector came on the excitement quickly died down and all the players were filled with a somber reality. We were going to play, at that time, the best Division II team in the nation. And without a doubt, the best team we had played all year. The offensive line was the biggest we had faced. The Sioux had led the nation in rushing. Running behind the big offensive line was 6'3"

212-pound fullback Bill Deutash who was the third leading ground gainer in America with an average of 129.9 yards a game and Dale Kasowski a 6'3" 215-pound tailback who was the fourth leading rusher in America averaging 122.9 yards a game and who also, at the time, the leading scorer in America. By comparison, I was 6' 215 pounds and only one other defensive starter was bigger than me.

Some other crushing news was that we would be without four defensive players. Two starters, and two reserves that played significant time in every game. One of those was Stanley King who would later be named the GSC Defensive Player of the year and who had set a record with 10 interceptions and was also among the leading tacklers. Why? All four had been eligible by NCAA to play in the regular season, but as typical as you would expect from the NCAA, three of the four had not been at Livingston for "one year and 24 hours" and the other had been redshirted his freshman year. I had been redshirted my second year because I did not play and was eligible. My opinion of these rulings was that someone in the NCAA bureaucracy had to much time on their hands. All four should have been eligible for the playoffs if they had, by NCAA rules, been eligible in the regular season. They made the trip with us but all four were heartbroken.

It was Thanksgiving week and most of the students had left campus. We practiced Monday, Tuesday, and Wednesday on the game field. That gave us a lift in spirits. Coach King was a master at looking for the little things that would give us an edge in any game and one of the ways was the comments he was making to the press. He had told us not to believe what we read but he was telling the press, "that he hoped that we wouldn't get embarrassed", "that ND could play with a lot of Division one schools, (in fact, Minnesota, from the Big Ten, had only beaten them 40-30 the year before)", "Y'all got better folks", "I (King) could average 6 yards a carry behind that(ND) line", etc. We expected as much from him, but we also knew that he fully expected us to compete with the Sioux and to beat them if we got a few breaks.

I do not know how much his words went toward making the North Dakota players and coaches overconfident. Being 9-0, ranked number 1 in the nation, playing against an unranked team from the middle of the Black Belt in Alabama, probably had already given them a big dose of overconfidence.

But what really contributed to their overconfidence and what also gave all of us associated with Livingston and edge of determination, anger, and a feeling of disrespect was a headline and article in the University of North Dakota student newspaper.

LIVINGSTON WHO?

The editor of the newspaper probably did not check with the North Dakota head coach before he gave permission for the story to be written as such, but he should have. It gave us a rallying call at practices and was constantly playing in our minds. “Livingston Who”, “Livingston Who”, Livingston Who”. We might not beat them, but they were at least going to find out WHO “Livingston Who” was.

Our itinerary was to fly to Grand Folks, North Dakota on Thanksgiving Day and have two short practices on Friday before the 12:30 kickoff on Saturday. We had a smooth, quiet, and enjoyable flight to Grand Folks. We went to our hotel and then had a great Thanksgiving meal. Other than not having any grits in Grand Folks the food was excellent. One thing we did notice after landing, boarding the buses, and going to the hotel was the weather. It was around 5 degrees F. The creeks were frozen and the slight bit of snow that had fallen revealed footprints from people walking over the frozen water. He also saw something even more remarkable. People were outside working. In fact, there was a crew of workers replacing a roof on a building across from our hotel. We had excellent hosts everywhere we went, and they would tell us to “please talk some more, we love to hear your accent.” They were not making fun of our Southern drawl, they just truly wanted to hear it.

On Friday we had practices outside of the stadium scheduled for 10 a.m. and 2 p.m. I wondered why we had two practices schedules, but I soon found out. The temperature had warmed up to 8 degrees F. We were in our “warm-ups” but about all they did was to keep us from getting frostbite. We practiced for 30 minutes each time. We went over some things the second practice that we did not go over the first practice. 30 minutes was literally all we could stay outside. We made a mad dash for the bus each time practice was over trying to warm up as fast as possible. We got very little accomplished as far as game assignments were concerned, but we did begin to get acclimated to the weather. I do not know whose decision it was for us to travel on Thursday and stay two nights before the game, but it was genius. Although we got very cold fast, we also had time to prepare our minds for the cold while we were inside. If we had flown up on Friday, I believe the weather might have been something we could not have overcome. Coach King kept making the point over and over that “they have to play in the same weather as you. Which ones are going to rise to the occasion?”

After dinner that night we were treated to something none of us had ever experienced, an ice hockey game! North Dakota was a powerhouse in NCAA hockey, and it was exciting to see this sport in person. In my opinion ice hockey players, as a whole, are the best athletes in any sport. I believe that someone trying to hit a baseball from a major league pitcher is the hardest single skill in the world of sport, but think about skating forward and backwards, on a single blade, at high speed, wearing several pounds of equipment, crashing into walls and opponents, all the while trying to maneuver a "puck" that is one inch thick and three inches in diameter with a three foot stick, and having the goal being to put it into a net guarded by a player that is almost as large as the opening! Anyway, we stayed until sometime into the second period before going back to the motel for the night. We would have an early rise with a 12:30 kickoff time and we needed to start focusing on the challenge ahead of us.

We had an early breakfast and a short team meeting. We arrived at the field which was covered by flax straw to keep it from freezing. It did not work plus there was also a cover of snow on it. More snow was predicted as a winter storm watch had been issued. I am pretty sure a winter storm watch is more serious in North Dakota than Alabama most of the time. However, there was some good news. The temperature had risen to 28 degrees F! We went inside our locker room and took turns getting ankles taped and other medical issues tended to. We had a great athletic trainer in R.T. Floyd who came to Livingston as basically a "walk-on athletic trainer assistant", but who is now Dr. Floyd earning his doctorate from the University of Alabama, who has served the University of West Alabama for 47 years and has the athletic training facility named after him. I got both ankles taped and my left hand padded and taped from breaking it during the Tory State game earlier in the year. Silence filled the locker room. Concentration was at an all time high. Coach King paced the room, making eye contact and nodding, but not saying much. We also would be doing two things different for this game. One would be going out later than normal for warmups, which would be shorter than usual. The other was a uniform addition. Every player had brought a pair of thermal underwear to wear. This was not new for cold weather games. The thermals would help with the cold, but since they were made of cotton they could contribute to the cold if a player was a perfuse sweater and the thermals held the water in on the body. To have an extra layer of warmth and prevent the sweat from making a person colder, the coaches passed out our secret weapons, plastic garbage bags! They gave us baggies for our feet and full-size bags for our upper body. We put the baggies over our feet and then put our socks on. We then poked holes in the large bags for our arms and head to fit through which covered the torso. We then put on our uniforms on and felt like we had scored an early touchdown against the Sioux.

After warmups we came back into the locker room for some last-minute instructions. There was not a giant, fiery speech by Coach King, just a short reminder for us to play every play with intensity, play like we had all year, bend but don't break and take care of the football. After the Lord's Prayer we headed for the David v Goliath match.

We scored two early touchdowns to take a 14-0 into the second quarter. The Sioux would score two touchdowns to tie the score at halftime, but we had turned them away from other scoring opportunities. Leaving the field, we felt emboldened and had a sense that the North Dakota players had not mentally prepared for the game as they entered their locker rooms with their heads down.

There was not a lot of talk, hollering, or moving around inside the locker room but our confidence was growing. The offensive and defensive coordinators made what adjustments that were needed. Coach King said, "30 Minutes", "give all you have for 30 minutes, and you will come back in here victorious"!

The third quarter was back and forth exchanges of punts until our defense stopped a North Dakota drive on our 23. The offense put in a sustained 77-yard drive that ended with QB Ricky Seale scoring from 8 yards out. We were ahead again and this time we would not relinquish it. After stopping the Sioux again and making them punt, the offense took over on the 20-yard line. They would score again, but not with a sustained march. Instead QB Willie Slater took it around right end and 63 yards later he was in the end zone. Slater looked so fast on the play that it seemed as if he was the only one moving. The game was "over" at that point. We would add an additional touchdown to make the final score 34-14.

North Dakota had the size, but we had the speed. The speed was obvious on the offense, but our defense, other than the tackles and nose guard, were as fast, or faster, than their two large running backs. We bent a lot but held most of the first half. In the second half we did not bend very much, and North Dakota had only one scoring threat.

Not only was our offense fast, but the offensive coaches, along with Coach King had installed the no-huddle offense. When I say no-huddle do not think about the no-huddle offenses that today's college teams run. After the football was placed ready to play by the official the offense would line up on the ball. The QB would have already called for the formation before the spotting of the ball so by the time the ball was spotted all the offensive players were in a position for the ball to be snapped. It was not a hurry-up offense, but they could snap it at any time. They had code words that would tell the offense to run a predetermined play if the defense relaxed in any way. If the defense was in their ready to play position and remained there the QB would call the play that was signaled in from the sideline, all the while with his hands under the center ready for the snap. This offense made it a little harder, mentally, and physically, for the defensive teams. Teams in the North did not see many wishbone offenses and North Dakota was one of them. They only had a few days to make a scheme and learn it, but it did not help much as our offense outgained the Sioux's offense, including outrushing them.

The few fans that had made the 1,100-mile trip were delirious. In the group of fans was my father that had flown in the night before. In all my high school and college career he only missed one of my games, a game in which I was dressed out, but was not expected to play because of an injury. However, it was not a giant celebration after the game. The celebration started after Salter's run and continued for the remainder of the game. After the game everyone was ready to get warm.

It was one of the greatest games most people never seen. The odds of Livingston beating North Dakota were very low. But a game like this is what makes football great. It was a TEAM victory. I know that term is used a lot, but that is what we were in 1975, a team. A team that cared for each other. A team that cared about winning.

Finally, one of the headlines after the game was:

"DAKOTIANS KNOW "WHO", NOW"

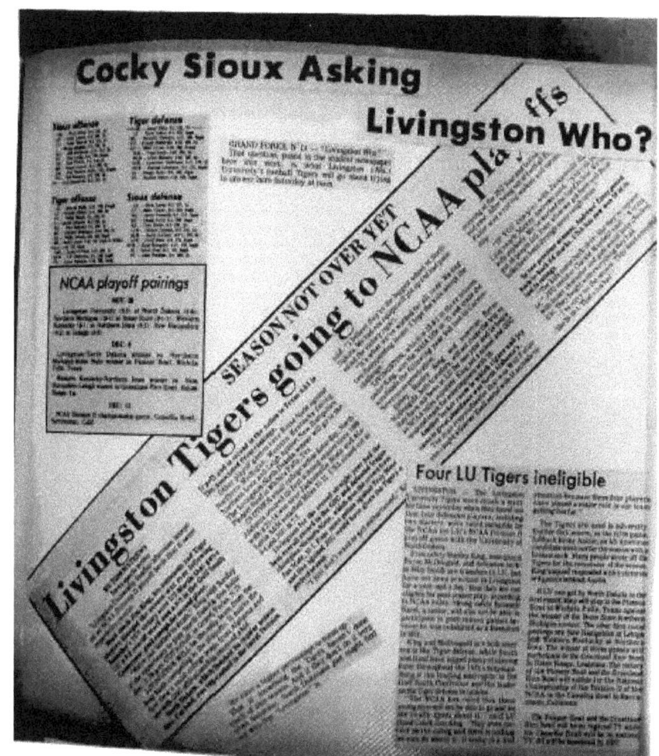

Cocky Sioux Asking Livingston Who?

SEASON NOT OVER YET

Livingston Tigers going to NCAA playoffs

NCAA playoff pairings

Four LU Tigers ineligible

There were questions before the game, but they were answered during it.

My biggest fan

LIVINGSTON FAN--Leon Pitts has to be one of the greatest football fans around. He went to North Dakota this weekend to see Livingston top highly regarded and favored University of North Dakota 34-14 in the NCAA division II playoffs. The temperature at the game was two degrees. But he had good reason to be an avid fan his son Jerry is a standout on the LU team. Here, Mr. Pitts displays a paper he picked up in North Dakota and a down marker from the playing field.

Chapter 11

The Hand Of GOD

The Hand of God

Events that take place in a person's life, especially those that were dangerous, are often referred to as being "lucky" in the instance that things did not turn out worse. I used to think that way. However, I now know that it was not luck involved but the Hand of God watching over me. I am sure there are several instances that I do not recall in which the Hand of God protected me from a much worse fate than what happened but there are enough to know that I am still alive because of the Grace of God.

RATTLESNAKE: Growing up in the country meant there was always a chance for snakes to be close by. We never encountered many in our yard, probably because for years we had a cocker spaniel who was fearless when it came to attacking snakes. "Nippy" was covered with thick, black hair and was blessed with quick reactions. Once he had the snake in his mouth it was over. He would shake it violently, throw it down, pick it up and shake some more. He would repeat this process until the snake was dead. However, he often paid the price for these encounters when it came to poisonous snakes. Several times he would show up with a swollen face and we knew he had been bitten by a poisonous snake. My mother would force used grease down his throat as a method to counter the poison. He recovered every time and lived to fight another day. That dog lived to be over 12 years old. One day we noticed he was missing. We never saw him again.

The county was completely redoing the road that was located by our house. The previous one was very crooked with a lot of hills and valleys in it. As this construction was proceeding it brought giant machines, in my eyes, as I was only ten years old at the time, and a lot of dirt before they paved it. One afternoon, after a heavy rain, the construction area was a mud pit. A great chance to get bare footed and enjoy the outdoors. After several minutes of wondering through the mud and around the bulldozers I decided I had enough. The back of our house had a spicket with a water hose. A perfect place to wash off the mud. Just as I completed the task and turned off the water I turned and there it was. Three feet from me, in striking position, was the rattlesnake. Stunned, I froze, which was probably the best thing that I could have done. I looked at it for a few more seconds and then was able to break to the side, away from the snake and kept running until I was inside the house. My father came out and killed it. If I had backed up any after turning the water off or had just causally walked away from the spot I was at, the odds are I would have surely been bit. With the roads being muddy and the doctor several minutes away and at a place that might or might not have had any vaccines, the situation would have been grave. I believe the Hand of God caused me to turn around in the spot I was standing and made my eyes see the snake before I moved which probably saved my life.

MIDNIGHT TRAIN: My early social life involved hanging out with my guy friends. Usually eating at the same two places in Sulligent and an occasional trip to Amory to play pool or to Columbus to watch a movie. These trips were rare and most of our free time was spent in Sulligent. The immediate close circle of friends included Carlos Flynn, Mike Knight, Jimmy Ray, and me. We all started dating girls about the same time during the early part of our junior year in high school. I had a female cousin who lived in Columbus who was about a month older than me. Sandra and I had always been close as for most of her life she had lived within a half mile of me, we were in the same grade, and we had spent summers together with our grandmother. I cannot remember the exact circumstance that caused me to set her up on a date with another close friend of mine, Mike Mixon, but I convinced her to go out on a date with him. Her parents agreed to it, but only if I went along so that it would be a double date. Sandra found a nice friend of hers to go out with me and we were set. Everything went well. Mike and Sandra started dating on a regular basis and I would double date with different friends of Sandra's. I eventually met one girl that we started dating regularly also.

The real story her is that Columbus was over thirty miles from Sulligent and that it took about 45 minutes I those days to get there. Mike and I would swap driving every other time when we would go there. When Mike would drive my hose would be on the way to Columbus, so he did not have to go out of his way any to pick me up. However, when it was my time to drive, I would have to go about eight miles from my house, on the other side of Sulligent to pick him up. Although the girls always had a curfew of eleven p.m., that still meant that Mike and I would get back home around midnight.

I lived in the country and so did Mike. The difference was that a person had to cross over a set of railroad tracks to get to Mike's house. After a person turned off the main highway on to the country road heading to Mike's the elevation of the land took a significant drop. Because of this drop the railroad tracks had been built up on an elevated foundation. The elevation was about four feet higher than the normal elevation of the land around it. The railroad company had done a good job of making the crossing a smooth event and a person driving over it would not have to slow down very much to do so. However, there were not any electronic warning signals or barrier arms that would come down when a train was approaching. There was only the standard sign that had

X shaped arms and the words "railroad crossing" written on it. When approaching the crossing a person could see a significant way both to the left and right of the tracks. However, by 1970 railroad travel and business on the train tracks that went through Sulligent had declined. This meant that a person crossing the tracks rarely encountered a train. This led to a decreased awareness of the danger that was presented at these types of crossings and an almost never stopping and looking down the tracks to see if a train was approaching.

Mike and I were returning from Columbus after having a date. It was my turn to drive and I had just dropped him off at his house. It was late, approaching midnight. I was very tired. We had a football game the previous night and it was usually two days after a game that I would be fully recovered. This had been a long day and night and I was ready for bed and rest. Surprisingly, I was not driving fast but kind of in cruise mode. Usually, I would have been driving above the speed limit to get home and into bed as fast as possible. I would never stop at the railroad crossing because in all the times that I had been to Mike's I had never encountered a train. This night, on my way home, without looking right or left, I stopped at the base of the crossing. At the exact same time that I came to a stop a train sped by in front of me. I saw its giant light beaming out as I stopped. I never heard a warning sound from it, just a flash and there it was. It is hard to tell how fast a train is moving as opposed to telling how fast a car is moving, but I have rarely seen trains go faster than what this train was going. When I had come to grasp what had just happened, I put the car into park and sat there in a stunned realization of what had just happened and what could have happened.

The Hand of God had changed my usual routine. He had slowed me down and made me do something completely different by me stopping the car. My usual routine would have been to drive up on to the tracks without looking. I may have made it across the tracks safely, but I also could have been on the tracks and been hit broadside by the train or I could have approached the train and without the benefit of any lighting, other than my headlights, drove into the side of the train. The whole event was very frightening, and I just sat still in my car for several minutes after the train passed. I was thankful to be alive. I did not really understand why and what had just happened, but I know now that it was the Hand of God protecting me.

RECKLESS DRIVING: With my main pursuit in life was to be a great football player I had never smoked or drank any alcohol. I had bought in to the belief that to be the best you had to train like the best. However, I was around both drinking and smoking as both of my parents did and most of my aunts and uncles did. My parents were not heavy drinkers, but they did smoke heavily. They preached against both and I was convinced that what they said meant more than what they did. However, as with most adolescents, curiosity got the best of me during the summer before my senior year in high school. If you were 18 you could legally buy beer at that time. Beer was not sold in the county we lived in but was sold across the state line in Mississippi and was about twenty-five minutes to the first store that did sell it. I do not remember the first time we bought some and drove back to Alabama to drink it. I do remember we never got enough to get drunk but enough to be reckless.

My parents were out of town for the weekend, and when I say out of town, I mean South Alabama out of town. 6 hours away. We, a few other guys and I, decided we needed to have some beer to drink later that night. We would be able to drink it at my house without anyone bothering us. The problem was that we had decided to do this late in the day and that we also all had dates for that night. We did not want to be late for our dates, for obvious reasons, but we also did not want to go get the beer after our dates. I talked Carlos in to riding with me to get the beer before our dates. The car my parents had left me to use was powerful. Short on time I used that power to its fullest extent. The trip to get the beer was fine. Most of the trip back was fine. The only thing that was not fine was the lack of time and my judgement of the speed I was going. Doing 80 and 90 mph at times on the way back, on country roads, is never a good decision. We were about three miles from home and came upon a straight way. I gave it more gas. The best I remember is that I was doing around 90 when I see what was ahead of me. In the same lane as I was traveling was a truck, full of logs. It was what we call a "pulp wood truck". It had slowed almost to a stop and was begin its turn to the left to exit the road. Pulled off to the left side of the road, just barely on to the shoulder, were two cars. I do not know if that truck had broken down and those men, who were standing around those cars, were there to help or not, but it presented a huge problem to me. I realized I did not have enough time to slow down and stop. I realized that I could only go forward. Without letting up on the gas I passed the truck to the left without hitting it, the cars, or anyone standing around. We continued to my house, put the beer up, and then went on to our dates. Later we had an uneventful evening of drinking the beer and telling stories.

It was several years before I realized exactly how close I came, because of my reckless decisions, that not only did I almost end my own life, but the life of my friend and the lives of strangers. I had not even been drinking, but my ten-foot tall and bullet proof attitude had created a temporary monster of foolishness. The only reason I survived that situation, the only reasons those around me survived that situation, was the Hand of God. He slowed the truck down while it was turning. He kept the other men off the road. He guided my hands on the steering wheel as I passed all of them. God saved me again.

ALSEEP AT THE WHEEL: In 1969 if you wanted to work in the summertime between school years it was easy to find a job. It would usually be a labor job that required little in the way of labor skills. OSHA was still two years away and factories were in the business of making a profit and not too interested in the safety of their workers. Of course, working conditions were much better than 50 years earlier but there was still room for improvement.

After my sophomore year I was 16 and my mother was able to get me a job at her place of employment. She worked in what was commonly referred to as a "garment plant". The plant produced pants. From cloth, the patterns were cut, and then sent down an assembly line in which the workers specialized on only a part of the pants and then moved them to the next step in line. The last step was putting tags on the pants before shipping. My job was a "gofer"……go for this, go for that. Do this today, do something different the next day. I probably did at least a dozen different tasks that summer. It did pay minimum wage which was good money for me since my parents let me keep all that I earned. Some days were easy but most of the days were hard. Work time was at 7 a.m. and the company expected you to be wide open at that time. There was a morning break of ten minutes and an hour off for lunch. I had a much greater appreciation for the work my mother did after that summer. Her job was very difficult, both physically and mentally. She had to do a minimum number of pants each day to receive minimum wage but got a slight bump in pay if she did more. I was glad when it was time for football practice and school to begin.

After my junior year I did not want to go back to working at the factory again. I laid around the house a few days "looking" for a job. Nothing fell out of the sky and into my lap, but I was enjoying the time off. That ended when my daddy came to me and said, "find a job by the end of the week or next week you are going to start cleaning off ditch banks with a bushwhacker and sling blade. A bushwhacker had a sixteen-inch blade mounted on a four-foot-long wooden handle. It was used for heavy bush, limbs, and roots. A sling blade was much smaller and used for weeds. Understand that their function was completely controlled by the muscles of the person using it. There was not any type of motor attached to it. This would be a hard, hot, outside, and somewhat dangerous job, and there was the possibility that I would be working without pay, but I knew my daddy was serious and, with the help of my uncle, was able to find a job before the end of the week was up.

This job was at a double wide, fabricated home plant. This was a new concept at the time as only single wide homes were being built on a wide scale. My job was to cut 4'X8'X3/4" pieces of plywood down into four sections. To do this I would have to take the pieces and move them through a table saw that was slicing two-foot lengths the plywood. I would have four pieces of wood, which I would stack and then start with the next full piece.

When I had enough of these pieces to last through the shift, I would change my saw blades out so that I could notch partial holes in 2'X6"X12' pieces of wood that would be used for floor joists.

Both required hard labor and concentration. I did not have gloves, I did not have ear plugs, I did not have eye protection, I did not have a hard hat. OSHA was still a year away. It was so hard that when we had lunch, I would eat my meal as fast as I could and then go take a nap on top of a pile of plywood.

I did make more than minimum wage and it was also just what I needed to stay in shape and get stronger for the upcoming football season, so all in all, the first two jobs I had were blessings.

After graduation I had a busy summer planned before leaving for college. I planned to play with the high school baseball team in the summer league. I was playing in the Alabama High School All-Star game. I was working to try and save some money for expenses at college. The job I was able to secure was at a chemical plant in Aberdeen, Mississippi. It was about a thirty-minute drive from my house to the plant. The pay was a good bit above minimum wage. I soon found out why. The job I had required climbing stairs. About eight rungs to a platform with a forty-pound bag of chemicals. Opening those chemicals and dumping them into a large vat for the chemicals to be mixed. It required about ten bags of these chemicals for each project. This was the beginning of the making water hoses. When the chemicals were being dumped fumes from them would arise toward me and the entire room. Fortunately, this was a large area, and the fumes would disperse over the area instead of being concentrated. Over the years the fumes had settled on the overhead I beams causing them to look like triangles more than an upside-down T. Was this dangerous to my health? Of course, it was. Again, I did not have a breathing mask, no eye protection, no hearing protection, and no hard hat. The other major part of my job was to recycle water hoses that had defects in them. Water hose that had went through the process but had been inspected and determined not to be acceptable. The steps for this were simple. I used what was called "the hog".

In the middle of the floor there was a literal grinder that would shred the water hose so that it could be melted and used again. It had a circumference of about twelve inches with sections of metal teeth within it. Turning the machine on would cause the teeth to circulate so that when I would put the water hose into the grinder it would be shredded to very fine pieces. This machine was tremendously loud and did not have any safety features surrounding it. Remember, no OSHA yet.

This plant used a rotating sift for its workers. That meant that everyone would work the three different shifts over the course of a month. The shifts were from 8 a.m. to 4 p.m., from 4 p.m. to 12 a.m., and 12 a.m. to 8 a.m. These shifts were for a five-day period with a two day, sometimes three day, break in between the ending of one period of shifts and before the beginning of another. I never understood why this method was used by the management, but I hated it.

I had worked the 4 p.m. to 12 a.m. shift and the 8 am. to 4 p.m. shift and had just started the 12 a.m. to 8 a.m. shift for two nights. My aunt, uncle and cousin from Montgomery, Alabama came to visit us for the weekend. I had trouble sleeping during the day when doing the "graveyard shift", getting very few hours of true sleep. I enjoyed being with my cousin and instead of getting the sleep I needed, me and him went to a movie before my shift on that Saturday. I had not been at this particular job long enough to ask for a day off, so I went to work feeling good.

My daddy had bought me a new Ford Mustang Mach I in February. It was navy blue, with a stick shift, and it would fly. It was a big sacrifice on his part, but it was also a way to reward me and to show his appreciation for the things I had done and for the love he had for me. I was a pretty good driver, but like all teenagers I had my moments of bad decisions. None of those decisions had had any consequences to this point. After my shift was completed, I headed to my car feeling good, feeling awake. I had to drive about three miles from the plant before I had to take a turn on a different road. The sun was in my eyes and I was very relaxed in my car seat. The making of the turn is all I remembered before the accident, which occurred about five miles from that turn.

The road I was on now was mostly straight. However, there was this curve. I was awoken by loud noises. My eyes told me that I was still going forward but off the road on the left side and I was hitting small pine trees, two to three foot in height and small in diameter. This side of the road also was sloped at about and 80-degree angle and about ten feet deep. I reached for the steering wheel, but I blacked out. Shortly afterward, I was awake again. Not in shock, but confused, I realized the car was upside down and my body was on the top of the cab. Looking around, I realized that the engine was still running, so I reached up and turned it off. I then realized that the front of the car was pointing the opposite way that I had been driving. How many times it rolled over and how those rolls took place I do not know. I then realized that I did not have any pain, nothing felt broken, I was breathing good and I could move my limbs. I proceeded to roll down my window, which went up because of the car being flipped, and crawled out of the vehicle. A few feet from it I paused and just stared at it. Fortunately, there was not any smoke coming from it, but it was easy to see that the frame had been significantly bent from the rolling. I looked around and was surprised to see a house on the opposite side of the road. I walked over to the house, told the people there what occurred, and they let me use their phone to call my parents.

Evidently, I was so asleep and relaxed that my body just floated with the car as it rolled. The car was not equipped with seatbelts but since I was so big and the windows were up, and small, I had stayed in the car. It was probably a good thing that my body was able to move during the process as being secured to the seat might have resulted in serious damages. I went to the doctor as a precaution. I discovered I had a scratch on my forehead. That was it. I had muscle soreness for a few days afterward but that was all the medical issues that had resulted from the wreck. The car was totaled.

I did not survive that wreck because of some laws of physics that could be applied to my movement inside the car as it rolled. The crash, the rolls, the flipping, this was a death wreck. I survived because the Hand of God was over me. He still had a purpose for me and that was the only reason that I did not die that day on the side of that lonely Mississippi highway. The other purpose for the wreck was that God knew that if I had transportation when I went to college that I would not stay. My daddy could not afford to provide me with another car at the time. After a week at college and a week of shock at how college football life was, if I had still had the Mustang I would have left and came home, with or without permission. God knew my future had to send me through Livingston University and this wreck was more than just survival, it was a blessing.

JUST OVER THE HILL: My Uncle Llyod and Aunt Grace Morris were two of the sweetest and kindest people I have ever known. They would help anyone they could within their capabilities and would do it with love and compassion without thinking of getting something in return. They lived about a half of a mile from us. Their house was on top of a steep hill. Their driveway entrance was slightly down from the peak of the hill and on the left side of the road when going from my house to theirs. They were the first in the community to purchase a color television set. It was a large console with a larger than usual screen. With their location being on top of a hill they also got better reception than most other people in the community, especially us. They could get broadcasts from Columbus and Tupelo, Mississippi, and most of the time from Birmingham, Alabama. Because of this it increased the number of sports events that was available to watch. I remember the first football game I watched there. It was an NFL game, the room was dim, and the color seemed more vibrant then if I was watching it in person. It was one of my greatest experiences in my life to that point. They welcomed me with open arms any time I wanted to come and watch sports on it.

My daddy had purchased me another Ford Mustang. This one was not new but just as much fun as the other one. It was a 19966 Fastback model. It was bright yellow, but it had an automatic transmission instead of a stick shift. It was a more fun car the previous one I had.

The year was 1972 and I was living at home. I had a job with a company that put up metal buildings. My Uncle Lamar Pitts had gotten me this job as he was working with this company. The company was based in Columbus, Mississippi which meant leaving early in the morning to be at work by 7 a.m. Eventually, two other uncles, my father, and my best friend would be working for them. The reason that I was in this situation was that I did not go back to Livingston University in January after winter break. During break, at breakfast one morning, I told my parents that I was not going back. I was bracing for a war of sorts, but surprisingly, not a word or comment was said. I told them I was going to, what was called at the time, Northwest Junior College. The college is located at Phil Campbell, Alabama and was the first junior college in the state of Alabama. I had a friend who was attending classes there and we were going to commute together. The commute was over an hour, each way. My goal was to play on their baseball team. However, God had a say in this also so that my destiny would be fulfilled. The school ran on what was called a quarter system instead of semesters at the time. This meant that a shorter time frame would be used to get the same number of hours into a course as a semester would with the biggest difference was that most classes met every day in the quarter system. About three weeks into the quarter an announcement was made that the junior college would not have a baseball team that year. I was disappointed at this news. I felt like I was stuck on an island without any means of escape. I had too much time and money invested so I finished out the quarter and received credit for the classes I had taken. I realize now that if the college had fielded a team and that I had made the team I would have spent at least two quarters there and probably would have returned for a second year in the fall. If that had been the case, I never would have made my way back to Livingston University.

It was a beautiful Sunday morning. My mother usually fixed a "real breakfast" on Sundays. My father would go to town and purchase a Birmingham News newspaper which would be read over usually twice before lunch. The Atlanta Braves were going to broadcast their game that day, but on a channel that could only be seen on my Uncle Lloyd and Aunt Grace's television. I did not bother calling them to see if it was ok for me to come over. I knew that I would be welcomed, and they were not the type to stay inside on such a beautiful day. I told my parents where I was heading and got into the Mustang. I was making a leisurely drive to my destination.

BOOM! The sound rattled me as much as the force did. I did not know what had happened. I grasped the situation and discovered that I was not moving, that the front left side of my car was damaged, and I was at a complete stop in the road. I opened the driver's door, stepped out and then realized what had happened. About three hundred yards from me was another car in the ditch on the side it had been coming from. It was smoking some but as it turned out that was only from their radiator. I was not hurt. The other car had been traveling at a high rate of speed and when it came over the hill it was on my side of the road. My aunt and uncle were in their front yard when it had happened. As I was about to pull into their entrance, I noticed them and for some reason I paused. I paused because the Hand of God was protecting me. If I had continued and entered at the normal speed the other car would have hit me broadside and the result for have been devastating for me and both occupants in the other car. No one was hurt and the driver told us that he had veered back to his right just before impact. This resulted in a glancing blow that caused considerable damage to both cars. However, neither car was totaled. The Hand of God was not only over me that day, but also over the occupants of the other car.

THE DECISION: I was well into my job at Columbus at the middle of the summer. However, after five months of hard labor, I had made the decision to go back to college. This decision would not take me back to Livingston but to Florence, Alabama and to Florence State University, now known as the University of North Alabama. Again, I would try out for the baseball team. The Hand of God was over me in this decision also. I had not played baseball in over a year. I had been an above average catcher and hitter in high school and was still in great physical shape. However, God placed two, not one, but two. Junior college All-American catchers on that team as newcomers. I went through fall practice with them but did not get much playing time and I knew that I would have to make another decision.

Those are not the decisions that I am focusing on in this segment. It is the middle of summer and my Uncle Lloyd is doing some remodelling at his house. He is planning on going by a hardware store after work on his way home to pick up some materials. He asks me to ride home with him just for company and to help him load and unload his materials. We out of the way of our normal way home to get the materials. The main thing he is getting is eight 2'X6"X12' planks. We are in his pickup truck. Evidently, he underestimated how long the planks would stick out of his truck even with the tail gate down because they were sticking out several feet. He also forgot to bring any straps to bind them together. He stacks the planks in two sets of four high. He decides that the best way home would be to go some backroads hoping that there would be less traffic than the main highway. We were about twenty-five minutes from his house when we started the journey. There was not any traffic on the road. About fifteen minutes into the journey the road turned from pavement into gravel. The truck started to bounce some on the gravel, not severely, but enough to make the planks to bounce slightly. I checked them once by looking through the rear window, but they had not moved much. A few minutes later my uncle asked to check them again. There was now a lot of movement, so much that one looked close to falling out. I also noticed, but did not think that it was an issue, that there was now a car behind us. The car was not close and did not seem to be driving fast. As my uncle pulled to a stop he did not pull to the side of the road. When the truck came to a stop I said, "I'll get it" and started to get out, but he was a perfectionist and said he would do it.

He exited the truck and at the same instant the door on his side of the truck slammed shut one plank came crashing through from the back. It came with such force that it went through the glass of a cab he had on the back of the truck, through the rear glass of the truck and through the windshield. About three feet of the plank was sticking out of the front of the windshield. The plank had also was sticking on the outside of the windshield. The plank had traveled directly over the steering wheel. Evidently, the person driving the car was not paying attention to us. He had slammed on his brakes but still slide into the plank which was at such an angle that it became a missile when he hit it. I had several pieces of glass in my arm, neck, and face. I was bleeding but it was only surface cuts as the glass exploded in small pieces. I was not in shock but was in state of confusion. I sat there and slowly turned to my left to see what seemed surreal. My uncle came running back to the cab to check on me. Once he knew that I was ok he too became stunned. The Hand of God had been over both of us that day. God made my uncle be the way he was so that he would get out of the truck to check on the plank. Had he stayed in the truck he would have been decapitated. God had his hand over me by directing the plank straight ahead instead of at an angle so that it did not hit me. All the timing, physics, dynamics of the driving of both vehicles, and other smaller factors that played into this incident could probably never be replicated. Because of the Hand of God everyone walked away from it unharmed.

BRIDGE OVER TROUBLED WATERS: By the summer of 1974 I had been back to Livingston for a year and a half. After a semester at Florence State University, I knew that I did not have a future in baseball, and I had just experienced my first year without playing football since the sixth grade. I realized I missed playing. I did not want to go out for the team at FSU. The head coach and several assistants that had been at Livingston were now at FSU. Two of the assistants I really did not like. I called a couple of SEC schools about walking on, but they told me that through I had missed the 1973 season I would have to red shirt the next year to become eligible. I started having conversations with my father about playing football again. Of course, this excited him. Without me knowing it, I guess because he did not want me to get my hopes up and the plan he had not materialize, he had called Clemit Spruiell at Livingston. Clemit was also from Sulligent and was quarterback on the state championship team of 1966. I was an eighth grader on that team and Clemit was a person to look up to. Clemit was also the senior quarterback who led Livingston to the National Championship in 1971, my freshman year. My father asked Clemit to see if there would be a chance for me to return to Livingston. Jim King, who was offensive line coach in 1971, had become the head coach. He did not coach me in 1971 but he knew me well as I played on the scout team against the first team offense. One night in January my father told me what was going to happen. He told me to expect a phone call later. The call came and it was Clemit on the line. He asked me if I was serious about coming back and a couple of other questions. I told I was and then he said, “Coach King wants to talk to you”. Coach King was very direct, but not intimidating. He asked about my goals and how sincere I was about wanting to play again. I convinced him I was ready. He said, “be here in two days and you will have a full scholarship waiting on you”. I was there in two days. The result of that conversation, that had been orchestrated by my father, saved my future and the quality of life I would lead.

When I arrived and as I went through spring training and early fall practices before the 1973 season began, I could tell how much I had lost in my football ability. However, as time passed it all started coming back and I was a starting outside linebacker by the seventh game of the season. I had a great off season and spring training. I was in the best shape of my life and was looking forward to my junior season. I was also married.

In 1974 most college football players did not stay on campus during the summer like most do today. I was one of the few who did because since I was married, I did not want to give up my on-campus apartment. There was more free time to enjoy and on one beautiful day another married player, Ricky Seale invited us to go with him and his wife on a picnic. He said he knew the perfect spot. The spot turned to be a bluff overlooking the Tombigbee River and was beside a railroad. I have always enjoyed trains but even more so when they cross over a river. However, I did not have the feeling that I would be fortunate to see one during our trip, so I did not get my hopes up. The bluff and railroad were about forty feet above the river. The Tombigbee River was very deep at this point and it was flowing swiftly.

After eating, talking, and tossing a football around some on the bluff, Ricky and myself decided we needed a little more activity. There were not any cell phones, social media, or other outside distractions at that time. But there was a railroad track and bridge. As we headed toward the tracks, both of our wives became anxious and telling us not to go on them. Of course, we did not pay any attention to them. The tracks were about 7 or so feet lower than the bluff we were on. We first took small steps getting a feel of the environment around us. As we approached the first part of the bridge that had the river beneath us, the warnings from the bluff became louder. Ricky and I just smiled at each other without acknowledging the warnings.

The railroad bridge that was over the river covered about 150 feet. However, it was not like most railroads in which you can see for a long distance as it had a sharp curve about 50 feet after the end of the part that was over the river. We had now progressed out to around forty feet on the bridge over the river. We had stopped to look at the river and, of course, to spit into it to see how long it would take for the spit to hit the surface of the river. Ricky was on one side of the railroad tracks and I was on the other. This setup, and the fact that we had paused our journey, proved to be important. Leaning against some of the metal I became aware of a noise. I looked at the other end of the bridge and there comes a train, wide open! On instinct, we both started sprinting toward the bluff. Both wives were standing and screaming. I was on the side of the bluff, but Ricky would have to cross over the railroad tracks to go up it. The train was sounding its warning horn as I am sure the conductor knew it would be useless to try and stop such a powerful machine going full speed. Neither of us looked back until we got to the top of the bluff at which time the train roared by with another warning blast from the conductor as he shook his fist at us. I am sure he was as scared as we were.

We had missed our death by a few seconds at the most. While on the bridge we could not jump into the river and survive or try to hold onto the metal beams as the force from the train would have surely sucked us into it. The only option was to run. The Hand of God was over us in that he had prepared us for this moment by being great physical shape and having the athletic ability that we possessed. The Hand of God had paused our journey over the bridge that kept us from going a distance that would have been too far for us to have safely made it back to the bluff. The Hand of God kept us upright as we raced down the railroad tracks because any stumbling would have resulted in our death. Ricky and I tried to act like what had happened was not a big dal as our wives fussed on us unmercifully. But it was a big deal. The big deal was that the Hand of God had saved us.

SLIP SLIDING AWAY: Like any other summer I had a job to make extra income. I had a job that I had a love/hate relationship with. In 1974 the state of Alabama, like a lot of other states, was in the process of building an interstate road system. Just a few miles outside of Livingston, Interstate 20 was being built. Since it was summer the project was being worked on 24/7 six days a week. My wife was a cosmetologist and the person she worked for had a husband who was a foreman on the construction crew. Through this connection I was able to get hired with them. The job I would have was driving what was a packer, professionally known as a "sheepsfoot". It had large rubber tires on the rear, over which the cab sat and had a large round roller connected to the front of it. The roller had many rectangular lugs or "feet" which stuck out about six inches from the base. The machine had an automatic transmission that consisted of forward, park, reverse. It had power steering which you could make turns by using a finger. The roller was extended from the cab which made turning right or left easy. This model also had a grading blade extending beyond the roller.

My work shift was scheduled from 6 p.m. to 6:30 a.m. The night shift worked in two locations as a team. At one point wheel-tractor scrapers would be gathering dirt to bring to the point that I was working. When they got to my point, they would unload it while moving so that most of the dirt would be spread fairly over a large area. My job was to run over the dumped dirt as much as possible before the next load was delivered. I was told I could go back and forth, in circles, make figure eights, etc., just keep the machine moving on the dirt. I could even use the blade some if the dirt needed to be spread more than what the scrapers had left it. The experienced workers knew that I was about to experience extreme boredom. The operation went on at night as there were tall, bright floodlights located where the scrapers where digging, where I was located, and approximately hallway in between us. The scrapers and my machine were also equipped with lights. The project that we were working on was to build an earthen ramp for a road to go over the interstate. The reason for what I was doing is that the compaction of dirt on a potential new road must meet a certain specification before it can be surfaced. About every three hours an employee of the state road commission would drive to where I was working and put an instrument on the ground to measure the compaction. If it were to his satisfaction, he would give me a thumbs up, if not he would tell me what area needed more work.

A few weeks after the bridge incident I was in the middle of my ho-hum work shift. We had a thirty-minute break at midnight. I drove my machine away from the area I was working to take my break. After eating what I had prepared and after drinking some coffee I needed to relieve myself before going back to work. I had lowered the blade on my machine and had decided to step out on it and jump off instead of climbing down the side of it. As I lifted my left leg to jump and push with my right leg at the same time, my right foot slipped. Dew had built up on the steel of the front of the machine. I was able to go forward but not far enough. My left leg hit the top of the blade as I tumbled toward the ground. I was in severe pain for a while. After gathering myself I felt of my leg. It was not broken but there was an indention across my Tibia that is still there today. The Hand of God was over me in several ways at that moment. He kept my leg from breaking. If it had broken it I would not have played football that season and that setback would have probably ended my career and possibly my college education. The Hand of God allowed me to clear the blade with the rest of my body and to hit the ground instead of my head, chest or ribs hitting the blade and causing more damage, even death. At the time I thought it was both bad luck and good luck, but I realized eventually that it was the Hand of God keeping me on path to my destiny.

STOPPING AT THE BOTTOM: In 1976 I had my first professional job after graduating from Livingston University with a B. S. with a major in Physical Education and a minor in History. The job required me to teach physical education to grades k-6 during the school day and coach the varsity sports of football, basketball, and baseball in the afternoon. This meant I dealt with the mental range of age 5 to age 18 during the day. Part of the requirements of the varsity football job was to scout, evaluate, and have a game plan for the upcoming opponent. In today's world high school coaches can go online and get the video of their opponents. In 1976 games where still on film. Most coaches would swap game films directly with the coach of the other team. Most of the time a mutual halfway point between schools would be used to meet. Teams would keep those films all week and return them to their opponent on the next game night. Most teams would have the coaches on staff take turns to meet and swap films so that the task did not fall on the same coach each week. Once a coach had the films of their opponent, they were eager to get back to their offices and begin looking at what they faced the upcoming week. I was no exception. I had made the swap and was on my way back. It had been a rainy day and the roads were slick since it had been a while since it had rained in our area. As I was heading back, I was distracted thinking about our opponent. I was also going down a steep hill. Before I knew what was happening, I was almost at the stop sign. The road I was on had to stop because there was a road going in front of it and no road on the other side of the road I was on. I hit the brakes, but it was too late. I slide past the stop sign, through both lanes and stopped completely out of the road on the other side into the brush. I was not injured. The car was not injured. I was just stuck. Eventually, someone came by that had the ability to pull me out and get me on my way. What was the big deal? The Hand of God was over me in that there was not a car going either way that I hit or could have hit me. The Hand of God was with me in that there was not a giant oak tree waiting on me on the other side of the road. A lot of these situations happens with many people and they never think anything about other than it was bad driving, bad weather, or some other tangible factor that caused it without any injury to person or property. I say it is the Hand of God watching over someone even when the situation does not involve major damage or serious injury.

LOOK BOTH WAYS: IN the spring of 1989 I was living Jasper, Alabama and was employee, what was then called, Walker High School. I was an assistant football coach and the head baseball coach. I was single at the time and was renting a one-bedroom garage apartment. The location was about three miles from the school so I enjoyed the fact I could sleep in, get dressed I a hurry and get to school because that particular school my entire school day consisted of teaching physical education.

I have not ever had any true hobbies such as hunting or fishing. The only thing I have done on a consistent basis is to workout. It relieves stress, keeps the body in shape, and helps me mentally as I usually work out in the weight rooms of the school I have worked at which gave me solitude and allowed me to think.

I had recently purchased a new Ford Probe. I was really enjoying it. It was a great looking sports car, got high mileage, felt comfortable and handled well when driving. It was also in a good price range for me.

I had a monster workout. Usually, I do not overly push my body but on this workout, I had pushed it to the limit. I was heading home, exhausted, and ready for a hot shower. My path room took me through a few traffic lights, but mostly stop signs including some four way stops signs. Although, I was ready to get home I was not in any hurry. The last four way stop sign that I had to go through was on a hill. The road I was traveling was up and level, but the road I was crossing was a steep grade coming up from my right and continuing up to my left. Vision was good for everyone at all sides of the stop. I came to a complete stop. Looked both ways. I see a car coming from my right but knew it had to stop. As I pulled forward, I saw the car coming at a high rate of speed. I slammed on my brakes just before impact. ON impact my car started sliding and bouncing. I still maintained a firm grip on the steering and was still pushing with all my might on the brakes. After the car came to a compete stop, I was facing the direction in which I came. The other car had continued to go up the hill, for a bit but was sitting in a small ditch to the right. I exited my car, amazed that I was not hurt, and started inspecting the damage. Impact had taken place just to the right of my front tire. The person was speeding so much that the force from his car had spun me 180 degrees. I looked over at the other guy and a boy and girl were getting out. Also, an older lady was coming out of her house to look at the scene.

After the police arrived, she told them that she had heard the other car roaring up the hill. The police also found a whiskey bottle in the other car which still contained some whiskey. I had not even made my first payment on the new car. I was sad but not devasted. I had insurance coverage on the car and knew it would be replaced without a problem since the accident was not my fault.

The Hand of God caused me to slowly exit out through the four way stop and I had always been blessed with great peripheral vision and quick reactions. God had both prepared me for this moment and was there for me, and those in the other car. This had kept me from pulling out faster from the four stop which would have resulted in a broad side collision that could have killed all three of us involved.

THE CHINA VIRUS: In August 2020 I contracted the COIVD-19 virus, properly called the China virus because of its origin in China. I had the virus for a span of approximately three weeks. I do not know the exact day that it entered my body or the exact day it left, but from the first positive test until a negative test was around three weeks. I experienced about 10 rough days with days 6, 7, and 8, being the worse. My fever had spiked at 103 degrees Fahrenheit each of those nights. It had subsided some during each of the following days. At the beginning of night 9 my wife, Leslie, finally convinced me to go to the emergency room. I was tired of taking Ibuprofen and breathing treatments without any positive effects. At the ER I was given a cocktail mixture of medicines. I stayed there until my fever broke. It did not ever come back. It was two months before I regained my strength and energy. I know that sounds mild compared to what some people with COVID experienced, but it was also worse than what some people experienced. By day 9 I was seriously worried about the direction the COVID virus was taking me. I was approaching 68 years of age, a high risks category. The Hand of God kept death from coming for me. Part of the reason is that He had blessed me with good health most of my life, other than joint issues, and He had steered me to working out and staying in shape. I also believed He still had a purpose for me.

Summary: These are some of the events in my life that the Hand of God protected me from death or serious injury. There are others that I have chosen not to discuss, and I know there are some events that took place that the Hand of God was watching over me and I did not realize it. Think back in your own life at events such as these and ask yourself "was it just luck or was it the Hand of God"?

Jesus Christ is my Savior

Jesus Christ is the Son of God

Jesus Christ died on the cross for my sins and the sins of humanity, was buried in a tomb, and rose from the dead.

Jesus Christ will return to earth

If you repent of your sins, and ask God to save you, He will

Romans 10: 9-10

Chapter 12

Just the Facts

Introduction into the University of West Alabama Athletic Hall of Fame

Just the Facts

HIGH SCHOOL

FOOTBALL

6th, 7th, 8th, 9th Grades: Played on Junior High Team, Sulligent School

8th, 9th Grades: Played in JV games

8th, 9th, 10th, 11th, 12th Grades: Played in Varsity games

9th Grade: Started at Nose Guard

10th, 11th, 12th, Grades:

Started at Center

Started at Linebacker

Was Long Snapper on Punts

Was Short Snapper on PAT's and FG's

Was on Kickoff Return and Coverage Teams

Most Valuable Offensive Lineman

11th and 12th Grades

Most Valuable Defensive Player

10th, 11th, and 12th Grades

Honorable Mention All-State 2A

11th Grade

West Alabama Conference 1st Team

12th Grade

2A 1st Team All-State

12th Grade

Super All-State (All Classifications Combined)

1ST Team – 12th Grade

Scouting Systems of America All American

12th Grade

Led the team in Tackles

10th, 11th, 12th, Grades

Interceptions (Varsity)

1 – 8th Grade

2 – 10th Grade

6 – 12th Grade: 2 Returned for Touchdowns

Fumble Recoveries (Varsity)

1 – 9th Grade

2 – 10th Grade

3 – 11th Grade

2 – 12th Grade

1966 – Member of 2A State Championship Team (8th Grade)

1970 – Member of 2A Semi-final Team (12th Grade)

1971 – Participant in AHSAA All-Star Game

BASEBALL

Little League – 3 years

High School

Starting Catcher

10th, 11th, 12th, Grades

Selected to play in the East-West All Star game – 1971

12th Grade

Member of State Class 2A Runner-up Team

1971: 16-2, 12th Grade

Hit the first homerun and the first grand slam in the new field that was built by the town of Sulligent in 1970

BASKETBALL

Played on Junior High Team

8th, 9th Grades (Started 9th Grade)

Played on the JV Team

10th, 11th Grades (Started both Years)

Played on the Varsity Team

12th Grade: Started

LIVINGSTON UNIVERSITY

FOOTBALL

Member of the **1971 N.A.I.A. NATIONAL CHAMPIONSHIP** team

Lettered

Sophomore, Junior, Senior

Positions: Middle Linebacker, Outside Linebacker, Defensive End

Started in 7th game of sophomore season and started the rest of my career

SOPHOMORE

Interceptions – 2

Fumble Recoveries – 2

JUNIOR

Most Valuable Defensive Player

Led Team in Tackles

Interceptions – 2

Fumble Recoveries – 3

1st Team Gulf South Conference

1st Team Birmingham Post Herald Small College Team

1st Team N.A.I.A. District 27 Team

Most Dedicated Player Award

SENIOR

1st Team N.A.I.A. All American

A.P. Honorable Mention All American

1st Team Gulf South Conference

1st Team Birmingham Post Herald Small College Team

1st Team N.A.I.A District 27 Team

Gulf South Conference Player of the Week v Mississippi College

Elected Team Captain – Defense

Interceptions – 2

Fumble Recoveries – 2

City of Sulligent – Official Resolution

"Jerry Pitts Day" – December 24th, 1975

Who's Who in American Colleges and Universities - 1975

Outstanding College Athletes of America Member

1975

Livingston University Football Team of the Decade – 1970's

Defensive End – Elected by Peers

COACHING

BASEBALL

25 Years

23 – Alabama

19 State Playoff Teams

Class 2A Runner-up – 2001 – Sulligent High School

4X Coach of the Year

W-315 L-191

2 – Mississippi

Class 3A State Champions – 2007 – Nettleton

Coach of the Year 2007

W-48 L-22

TOTAL

W-363 L-213

SOFTBALL

1 Year

Sulligent High School

Class 3A State Runner-up 1986 W – 20 L - 8

FOOTBALL

Alabama

16 Years, Assistant Coach

2 Years, Head Coach

Georgia

1 Year, Assistant Coach

BASKETBALL

Alabama

3 Years Boys Head Coach

2 Years Girls Head Coach

6 Years Boys Assistant Coach

Wrestling

Georgia

1 Year, Assistant Coach

SEASONS COACHED

25 Seasons of Baseball

19 Seasons of Football

11 Seasons of Basketball

10 Seasons of Summer League Baseball

1 Season of Softball

1 Season of Wrestling

67 SEASONS TOTAL

OFFICATING

2 Years as AHSAA Football Official

STATE OF ALABAMA

OFFICIAL RESOLUTION

"COMMENDATION FOR A WINNING TRADITION"

2001

CITY OF SULLIGENT

CITY COUNCIL

NAMES CITY FIELD

"JERRY PITTS FIELD"

2004

LAMAR COUNTY SPORTS HALL OF FAME

Inducted 1989

UNIVERSITY OF WEST ALABAMA ATHLETIC HALL OF FAME

Inducted 2005

UNIVERSITY OF WEST ALABAMA ATHLETIC HALL OF FAME

1971 FOOTBALL TEAM NATIONAL CHAMPIONS - MEMBER

Inducted 2021

Above: Returning an interception against Nicholls State in 1973.

Right: My father congratulating me after winning the MVP on defense as a sophomore. That award inspired me to work harder to become a better player. I felt a burden of responsibility after winning it.

I was the Blue Devil's leading tackler for three straight years, but I always had a lot of help. 81-Mike Knight, 76-Joe Allen Jaggers, 25-Jimmy Ray, 77-Gary Turner, 60-Roger "Stump" Humbers

1975 1st Team All-American

1971 AHSAA All Star Game Participant

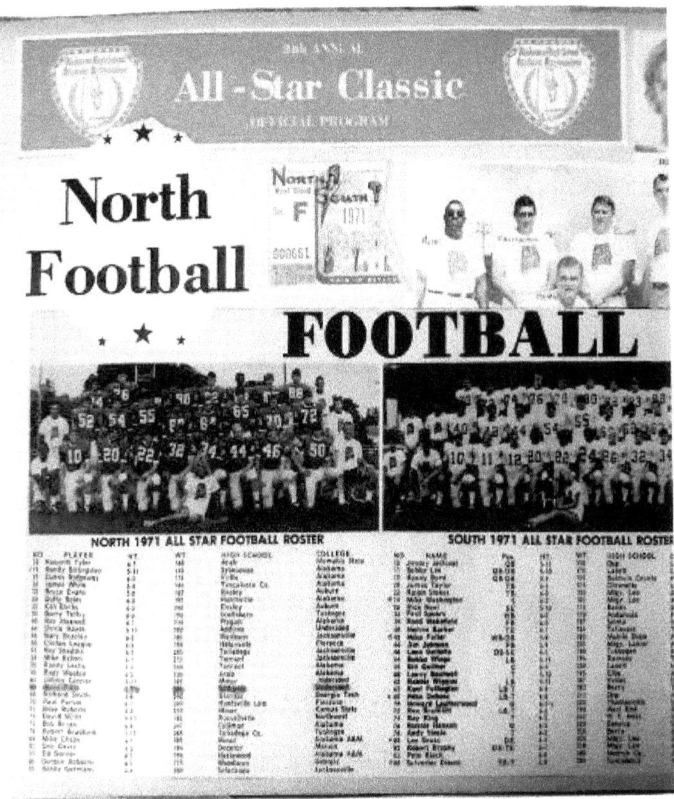

Inducted into the LU Tigers Football Team of the Decade 1970-79

City of Sulligent Proclamation: December 14th, 1975 "Jerry Pitts Day"

My all-time favorite player, my son, Nathan Pitts, at his first baseball game and later surprising me with a return on what would be my final home game at SHS

Finesse and Brawn: My daughter, Ashley was a high school All-American cheerleader and also a State Champion Powerlifter.

www.ingramcontent.com/pod-product-compliance
Ingram Content Group UK Ltd.
Pitfield, Milton Keynes, MK11 3LW, UK
UKHW051138260726
13967UKWH00010B/3122

9 781088 195826